A
Dwelling Place
Within

D0906006

The Saints Speak Today Series

Let Nothing Trouble You
St. Teresa of Avila

Restless Till We Rest in You
St. Augustine

A Dwelling Place Within
St. Francis of Assisi

Be Merry in God
St. Thomas More

THE SAINTS SPEAK TODAY

A Dwelling Place Within

60 Reflections From the Writings of St. Francis

COMPILED BY
MARY VAN BALEN HOLT

CHARIS

SERVANT PUBLICATIONS
ANN ARBOR, MICHIGAN

© 1999 by Servant Publications
All rights reserved.

Charis Books is an imprint of Servant Publications especially designed to serve Roman
Catholics.

The English translation of the Psalms from the *Liturgical Psalter* © 1994,
International Committee on English in the Liturgy, Inc. All rights reserved.

Servant would like to thank the following publishers for permission to excerpt the following works: Excerpts from *The St. Francis Omnibus of Sources,* © 1983, used by permission of Franciscan Press. Excerpts from *Penguins + Golden Calves,* by Madeleine
L'Engle,© 1996, used by permission of Harold Shaw Publishers. Excerpts from
Showings, by Edmund Colledge and James Walsh, eds., © 1978, used by permission of
Paulist Press. Excerpts from *St. Francis of Assisi,* by G.K. Chesterton, © 1957, used by
permission of AP Watt Ltd. Excerpts from *The Holy Rule of Our Most Holy Father
Saint Benedict,* edited by Benedictine Monks of St. Meinrad Archabbey, copyright
1975, used by permission of Abbey Press. All rights reserved.

Servant Publications
P.O. Box 8617
Ann Arbor, MI 48107

Cover design: Left Coast Design Inc., Portland, Oregon

99 00 01 02 10 9 8 7 6 5 4 3 2 1

Printed in the United States of America
ISBN 1-56955-074-3

Dedication

To Rick, Joshua, Emily, and Kathryn,
and all who strive to balance
the love of nature, the demands of life,
and the needs of the spirit.

Contents

Take Up Your Cross

Called to Be Servants

Creation: A Ladder to God

Filled With Praise and Joy

Acknowledgments

I would like to acknowledge those who have helped bring this book to completion. A number of people lent me materials to use as I researched the life of St. Francis of Assisi. Father Jack Maynard was generous with his library of books and videos. They proved invaluable. Mary Good's contribution was timely and helped my spirit as well as the project. Howard Distelzweig's interest in Brother Charles de Foucauld provided me with material and introduced me to a man who preached by his presence and example among unbelievers as Francis desired to do. Peter Distelzweig helped by scouting Notre Dame's library.

Besides providers of books and information, I had support from family and friends. My children once again assumed added responsibilities and shared their mother's time and attention with the demands of writing a book. My husband offered encouragement and belief in the project as well as more help on the home front.

Many hands help with the production of a book. I would like to thank everyone at Servant Publications, especially my editor, Heidi Hess. Her flexibility as well as her professional input are always appreciated.

Introduction

No matter where he was or what he was doing, St. Francis of Assisi had made *a dwelling place within* himself where his Lord God could stay. Whether preaching in the street or praying in solitude on the side of Mount La Verna, Francis could enter that quiet place in his heart and be at one with God. Known widely as the "nature saint," Francis' primary concern was for interior prayer in his own life and in those of his followers.

Instructing his friars to make their bodies a cell that they carried with them always, Francis had no difficulty combining contemplation and a life of action in the world. He was sensitive to God's presence and responded with his whole heart, at any time or place. This is encouraging for those of us who long for a life of prayer in the midst of the demands of a busy world.

Cultivating his dwelling place within was a lifelong process. Francis was in his twenties before he recognized the call to live for God alone. His life journey led him to embrace poverty and detachment from material things, though he deeply appreciated the created world. Scripture was his guide and inspiration as he followed in the footsteps of his beloved Savior. A faithful son of the Church, Francis made himself the least among men, the servant of all he met.

Although hundreds of years have passed since Francis traveled the roads of Assisi and surrounding countries, the wisdom of this medieval saint is still relevant today. True to his admonition to "go through the world exhorting all men and women by our example as well as by our words," much of what St. Francis has to teach is found in his life rather than in his written word. Reflecting on his rich spirituality we will find insight to help us deepen our own.

About St. Francis of Assisi

In late 1181 or early 1182, St. Francis was born into the rugged beauty and political turmoil of Assisi, Italy. His devout mother, Pica, had him baptized "John." His father, Pietro di Bernardone, a cloth merchant, changed the name to "Francesco."

Growing up in a wealthy home, Francis had many advantages. His youthful ambition for knighthood and military glory was ill-fated, however. He was captured and imprisoned after his first battle, and returned home sick a year later. During his recovery, he found his former pursuits to be less satisfying. While his friends enjoyed parties, food, and song, Francis trailed behind, trying to understand the puzzling movement in his soul.

While on his way to join the Crusades, Francis had a dream. God spoke to him, revealing the folly of his desire for a military career. Francis returned home and became increasingly solitary, seeking remote places where he could pray.

One day while riding near Assisi, Francis came upon a leper standing in the road. Francis had always avoided the leper colonies on the outskirts of his town. Sickened by their diseased and rotting flesh, he turned away from the afflicted. But this encounter would be different. It was a turning point in his conversion. Something within his soul moved him to leap off his horse and embrace the poor leper. Placing coins into the man's hand, Francis pressed his lips against the diseased flesh and kissed it. Suddenly, what had been repugnant to him became sweet. Having conquered himself and followed God's command to love the least of men, Francis experienced a change of heart. As he rode away, his joy overflowed into songs of praise.

Some time later, while praying in a small country chapel called San Damiano, the painted figure of Christ on the crucifix spoke to him: "Francis, go, repair my house, which, as you see, is falling completely to ruin." With characteristic enthusiasm, Francis took the command literally, sold some of his father's goods, and set about repairing the church. Later he would understand that the command encompassed the universal church. At that moment, however, Francis concerned himself only with the run-down chapel.

His actions enraged his father, who gathered relatives and neighbors to find Francis and bring him home. Terrified, Francis hid in a pit, eating food stealthily provided by a friend. Day after day, agony wrung tears and prayers from his soul. He ached to follow Jesus, yet was tormented by fears and uncertainty. At last, after a month had passed, Francis was infused with peace. He emerged confident of God's love and unwavering care. Returning to the city, he seemed oblivious to the jeering of those who watched.

The conflict with his father continued, culminating in a dramatic scene before the bishop and the townspeople. The young man stood before the crowd and gave back to Pietro not only his money but his clothes as well, declaring: "Until now I called you my father, but from now on I can say without reserve, 'Our Father, who art in heaven.' He is all my wealth and I place all my confidence in him."

Francis returned to San Damiano and continued his work. He begged for food and trusted in God's providence to meet his needs. Later, at a place called Portiuncula, in the chapel of St. Mary of the Angels, Francis listened to the Gospel and heard the words Jesus spoke, directing the apostles to go and preach, taking nothing with them. "This is what I long for with all my heart!" Francis exclaimed. From that moment his life had new direction. He made a crude habit and went out into the world, a barefoot preacher.

One by one, others joined him. By 1209 he had written a simple Rule for himself and his eleven companions. They set out for Rome to seek approval of Pope Innocent III. After prayerful consideration he blessed the order and told Francis to return when it had grown in numbers and grace.

Many were attracted to Francis and his little band. Clare, a devout young noblewoman of Assisi, joined Francis and his friars. Other women came to share her life of poverty and prayer. The Second Order of Franciscans grew from these beginnings: The Order of the Poor Clares. Married men and women and those not called to leave their life in the world also looked to Francis for spiritual leadership. Eventually he wrote a Rule for them and for those who would follow, becoming the Third Order of Franciscans.

By 1217 so many had joined Francis' order that the need for some organization became apparent. During the annual chapter meeting at Portiuncula the Order was divided into provinces, each having a "mother" or "custodian" to watch over it. Chapter meetings were held once a year and later, every three years. Francis used the gatherings to appoint new custodians, address his friars, and send them out to preach in other lands.

Always a missionary at heart, and longing for martyrdom, Francis traveled to Egypt, hoping to convert the Sultan. He was unsuccessful, but the Sultan was charmed by Francis and impressed by his faith and courage. Reluctant to have him leave, the Sultan asked for his prayers and had Francis safely escorted to the Christian camp. Distressed by the behavior of the Crusaders, Francis left the area and went to the Holy Land.

It was there that Brother Stephen found him in 1220 and brought news of division within the Order. Francis returned home immediately. The Order had expanded rapidly and included many clerics and scholars. The simplicity and poverty that had worked for twelve inspired men could not work for thousands. In Francis' absence some had tried to modify the Rule, particularly the adherence to absolute poverty. He appointed his good friend Cardinal Hugolin (later to become Pope Gregory IX) protector of the Order, resigned as minister general, and named Peter Catanii his successor. He wrote another draft of the Rule in 1223.

With an eye to the future viability of the Order, Cardinal Hugolin made some changes. Francis took the Rule to Rome. It was approved by Pope Honorius III. However, the discord within the Order remained a source of spiritual torment for Francis.

On his return from Rome, Francis stayed in the small town of Greccio. While there he wanted to celebrate Christmas in a way that would vividly recall the simplicity and humility with which Jesus entered into our world. With the help of a friend he transformed a mountain spot into a living tableau of the Nativity, complete with an ox and an ass. Christmas night was made bright by torches and candles carried there by the townspeople. Francis sang the Gospel and delivered the sermon. One man said he saw a child lying still in the manger and that it came to life when Francis picked him up. As Thomas of Celano recounts, "This vision was not unfitting, for the Child Jesus had been forgotten in the hearts of many ... but he was brought to life again through his servant St. Francis and stamped upon their fervent memory." Francis could not have known that his moving recreation would live on throughout the world in the tradition of the Christmas crèche.

Francis continued preaching, but his health, weakened by illness, fasts, and harsh treatment, was deteriorating. After the General Chapter of 1224 he was taken by donkey to Mount La Verna. There a hut was constructed near the hermitage. On September 24, 1224, the Feast of the Exaltation of the Cross, Francis was visited with a miraculous vision. While at prayer, St. Bonaventure writes, he "saw a Seraph with six fiery wings coming down from the highest point in the heavens.... Then he saw the image of a Man crucified in the midst of the wings, with his hands and feet stretched out and nailed to a cross.... As the vision disappeared, it left his heart ablaze with eagerness and impressed upon his body a miraculous likeness." Francis' hands and feet showed not only the wounds, but the likeness of nails, heads in his palms and on the tops of his feet and points protruding from the opposite sides. A gash split his side. Francis, who so closely resembled his Beloved in spirit, now resembled him in flesh as well.

Francis left La Verna on September 30, 1224, with Brother Leo and returned to Portiuncula. His body was tormented with illness, and his eyes had grown worse. On the way to see the Pope's physician at Rieti he stopped to see Clare. He was too sick to continue. Clare had a small hovel built beside the convent and cared for Francis. He could not endure the slightest light and kept his face covered most of the time. He was plagued by an onslaught of mice that filled the hut. They crawled over him and made sleep almost impossible. Overcome with suffering and tormented by the changes taking place in his Order, Francis cried out in agony.

Had God forgotten him? No. God promised Francis that his sufferings would be exchanged for a place in the heavenly kingdom, as surely as if Francis were already there. Francis was exuberant. In the midst of his pain, he composed the well-known hymn of praise, "The Canticle of the Creatures." It is considered one of the first great contributions to Italian literature.

As soon as he was able, Francis traveled to Rieti, where the area around his eyes was cauterized with a red-hot iron. In the spring Francis was moved to Siena for more treatment. His condition worsened. Brother Elias hurried to him. Sensing death's approach, Francis asked to be taken to Assisi.

Once at Portiuncula, he had himself placed in a little hut. He was laid, naked, upon the ground in honor of Lady Poverty. His brothers "lent" him some garments and placed him in a bed. Thinking that he should summon Brother Jacoba,* a noble

---

*Editor's note: Lady Jacoba, a dear friend of Francis, was sometimes called "Brother Jacoba" because of her strong and virile energy.

widow and friend who had given herself to the service of his Order, Francis began dictating a letter. Before it was finished she appeared at his door, saying God had revealed to her his impending death. She brought all that was necessary for his wake and burial, as well as the almond pastry he loved. Friday before he died he broke bread and passed it to those with him, as Jesus had done at the Last Supper.

On October 3, 1226, he had John's account of the passion read to him. According to his wishes, Francis was laid on the ground. He raised his feeble voice and intoned Psalm 141. The others joined in. When all was quiet they saw that Francis had ceased to breathe. At the age of forty-six, Francis had joined his beloved Savior.

A Final Word

This book is divided into sections that reflect different aspects of Francis' spirituality. Each day's readings are arranged around a theme and are designed to help you reflect on that theme from Francis' point of view. If read in the morning, the readings can resonate within you as you move through the day. An evening reading can help you to reflect on the day just past or set the stage for the one ahead.

This is not primarily a book about St. Francis. The intent is to help those who pray through it to look at God with Francis' guidance, allowing him to teach by his example how to live joyfully and fully in the service of our God.

A Dwelling Place for God

DAY 1
We Make Our Hearts a Dwelling Place for God

I bless God who teaches me,
who schools my heart even at night.
I am sure God is here,
right beside me.
I cannot be shaken.
So my heart rejoices,
my body thrills with life,
my whole being rests secure.

PSALM 16:7-9

MORNING READING

He selected the brothers he wanted to bring with him and said to them: "In the name of the Lord, go out two by two with becoming dignity; in the morning, observe silence until after tierce by praying to God in your heart. Let there be no useless conversation, for although you are travelling, your conduct must be as upright as if you were in a hermitage or in your cell. Wherever we are, wherever we go, we bring our cell with us. Our brother body is our cell and our soul is the hermit living in that cell in order to pray to God and meditate. If our soul does not live in peace and solitude within its cell, of what avail is it to live in a man-made cell?"

LEGEND OF PERUGIA

Accept, first, the solitude of your own heart. Prayer, like silence, is a matter of a journey inward, as are all pilgrimages of the Spirit. I must journey inward to meet the Triune God that dwells within me. To say all this may seem strange in the first chapter of a book which concerns, as you will soon see, a desert experience. But it is vitally important at the outset to emphasize that there is no need for a log cabin, cottages, huts, in order to lead a life of prayer. Prayer is interior. The hut, the log cabin, the chapel, is the human heart in which we must learn how to pray. Solitude sometimes helps prayer, and for special vocations is the cradle of prayer, and powerful prayer at that. But for the average Christian, prayer doesn't need a geographic spot. Prayer is a contact of love between God and man.

CATHERINE DE HUECK DOHERTY

FOR REFLECTION

My Companion God, how extraordinary that you chose to dwell so intimately within us. In the midst of daily life, help me remember that I have only to quiet myself and enter the deep places within my heart, to find you, waiting there for me.

EVENING READING

We should make a dwelling-place within ourselves where he can stay, he who is the Lord God almighty, Father, Son, and Holy Spirit. He himself tells us: *Watch, then, praying at all times, that you may be accounted worthy to escape all these things that are to be, and to stand before the Son of Man* (Lk 21:36).

THE RULE OF 1221

We Pray to Be Open to God's Direction

Search my heart, probe me, God!
Test and judge my thoughts.
Look! do I follow crooked paths?
Lead me along your ancient way.

PSALM 139:23-24

[Editor's note: Having been captured in battle between the warring cities of Assisi and Perugia, and kept prisoner for about a year, Francis was again ready to follow an Assisian nobleman into yet another military venture. After making preparations, Francis slept and had a vision of his home filled with armor and other trappings of war. Francis took this to mean he would accomplish great things in battle. Later, after setting out, he was visited in another dream by the Lord, who asked Francis why he was following another, lesser than the Master. Francis was instructed to return home where the Lord would make known his plans.]

MORNING READING

Changed, therefore, but in mind, not in body, he refused to go to Apulia and he strove to bend his own will to the will of God. Accordingly, he withdrew for a while from the bustle and the business of the world and tried to establish Jesus Christ dwelling within himself. Like a prudent business man, he hid the treasure he had found from the eyes of the deluded, and, having sold all his possessions, he tried to buy it secretly.

THOMAS OF CELANO, *THE FIRST LIFE OF ST. FRANCIS*

My Lord God, I have no idea where I am going. I do not see the road ahead of me. I cannot know for certain where it will end. Nor do I really know myself, and the fact that I think that I am following your will does not mean that I am actually doing so. But I believe that the desire to please you does in fact please you. And I hope I have that desire in all that I am doing. I hope that I will never do anything apart from that desire. And I know that if I do this you will lead me by the right road though I may know nothing about it. Therefore will I trust you always though I may seem to be lost and in the shadow of death. I will not fear, for you are ever with me, and you will never leave me to face my perils alone.

THOMAS MERTON

FOR REFLECTION

Lord, give me the wisdom to listen as you speak in my heart. Give me courage to follow the ways you make known to me. When I am not sure which path to take, give me a true desire to follow your will. Strengthen my belief that no matter what I do, you will bring all things to completion as you desire.

EVENING READING

Almighty, eternal, just and merciful God, grant us in our misery that we may do for your sake alone what we know you want us to do, and always want what pleases you; so that, cleansed and enlightened interiorly and fired with the ardour of the Holy Spirit, we may be able to follow in the footsteps of your Son, our Lord Jesus Christ, and so make our way to you, Most High, by your grace alone, you who live and reign in perfect Trinity and simple Unity, and are glorified, God all-powerful, for ever and ever. Amen.

LETTER TO A GENERAL CHAPTER

Scripture Is a Source of Spiritual Life

*"Yes," I said, "I will come
to live by your written word."
I want to do what pleases you;
your teaching is in my heart.*

PSALM 40:8-9

MORNING READING

In order that you may know how much Saint Francis approved of Bible-reading, let me tell you what I heard from a certain friar. He told me that when a copy of the New Testament was given to the brethren, and since it was impossible for them all to read it at once, Saint Francis divided it up into single sheets and gave one page to each brother, in order that all might study it and none interfere with another.

A NEW FIORETTI

In the sacred books the Father who is in heaven comes lovingly to meet his children, and talks with them. And such is the force and power of the Word of God that it can serve the Church as her support and vigor, and the children of the Church as strength for their faith, food for the soul, and a pure and lasting fount of spiritual life. Scripture verifies in the most perfect way the words: "The Word of God is living and active" (Heb 4:12), and "is able to build you up and to give you the inheritance among all those who are sanctified" (Acts 20:32; cf. 1 Thes 2:13). Let them remember, however, that prayer should accompany the reading of sacred Scripture, so that a dialogue takes place between God and man. For, "we speak to him when we pray; we listen to him when we read the divine oracles."

VATICAN COUNCIL II

FOR REFLECTION

Living Word, help me recognize the limitless source of grace you have placed in Scripture. Increase my love and desire for the glimpse of yourself that you share each time I come to you through your Word.

EVENING READING

When Francis was ill and filled throughout with pains, his companion once said: "Father, you have always sought refuge in the Scriptures, and they have always given you remedies for your pains. I pray you to have something read to you now from the prophets; perhaps your spirit will rejoice in the Lord." The saint said to him: "It is good to read the testimonies of Scripture; it is good to seek the Lord our God in them. As for me, however, I have already made so much of Scripture my own that I have more than enough to meditate on and revolve in my mind. I need no more, son; I know Christ, the poor crucified one."

THOMAS OF CELANO, THE SECOND LIFE OF ST. FRANCIS

God Listens to the Concerns of Our Hearts

God is my glory and safety,
my stronghold, my haven.
People, give your hearts to God,
trust always! God is our haven.

PSALM 62:8-9

MORNING READING

When the Friar Ministers urged him to allow the friars to possess something, at least, in common, so that so great a company might have some resources, blessed Francis called upon Christ in prayer, and took council with him on the matter.

MIRROR OF PERFECTION

In the midst of your work console yourself with him as often as you can. During your meals and your conversations, lift your heart towards him from time to time; the slightest little remembrance will always be very pleasant to him. To do this you do not need to shout out loud. He is closer to us than we think.

We do not have to be constantly in church to be with God. We can make our heart a prayer room into which we can retire from time to time to converse with him gently, humbly and lovingly. Everyone is capable of these familiar conversations with God—some more, some less. He knows what our capabilities are....

So make it a habit little by little to worship him in this way. Ask him for his grace and offer him your heart from time to time during

the day in the midst of your work—at every moment if you are able.
Do not constrain yourself by rules or private devotions. Offer him
your heart in faith, with love and humility.

BROTHER LAWRENCE

FOR REFLECTION

Lord Jesus, nothing is too small or insignificant to share with you.
Help me recognize you as Friend, always eager to know what is in
my heart. Have I kept quiet for too long? Increase my desire for
conversation with you.

EVENING READING

But when he prayed in the woods and in solitary places, he would
fill the woods with sighs, water the places with his tears, strike his
breast with his hand; and discovering there a kind of secret hiding
place, he would often speak with his Lord with words. There he
would give answer to his judge; there he would offer his petitions
to his father; there he would talk to his friend; there he would
rejoice with the bridegroom.

THOMAS OF CELANO, THE SECOND LIFE OF ST. FRANCIS

Quiet Prayer Balances Activity

Let morning announce your love,
for it is you I trust.
Show me the right way,
I offer you myself.

PSALM 143:8

MORNING READING

The man of God Francis had been taught not to seek his own, but to seek especially what in his eyes would be helpful toward the salvation of others; but above everything else he desired *to depart and to be with Christ*....

With fruitful devotion he frequented only heavenly dwellings, and he who had totally emptied himself remained so much the longer in the wounds of the Savior. He therefore frequently chose solitary places so that he could direct his mind completely to God; yet he was not slothful about entering into the affairs of his neighbors, when he saw the time was opportune, and he willingly took care of things pertaining to their salvation.

THOMAS OF CELANO, THE FIRST LIFE OF ST. FRANCIS

It is therefore obvious that those friars had effectively grasped the essence of the spirituality of St. Francis: the absolute unconditional primacy of the interior life, the life of ceaseless inner union with God, constant humble contemplation of the Savior, and intimate loving communion with him which the Poverello called "the spirit of prayer." And he repeatedly insisted that the various occupations of his friars should never be allowed to extinguish that holy flame in their hearts. Now it is evident that such a life can be lived in a hermitage in the woods or on a hillside better than anywhere else, as the contemplatives of all ages have found. It is also a little-known but significant fact that St. Francis himself founded and frequently resided in at least twenty-five such hermitages.

However, he also traveled and preached, not only all over Italy but even in France, Spain, Syria, and Egypt. His twenty-year apostolate was a continuous alternation between preaching tours and extended retreats in his beloved hermitages.

RAPHAEL BROWN IN
LITTLE FLOWERS OF ST. FRANCIS, INTRODUCTION

FOR REFLECTION

Jesus, help me balance the active and the quiet aspects of my life, recognizing both as a way of prayer. Give me grace to seek times of quiet contemplation to sustain me when my prayer is the work you give me to do in the world.

EVENING READING

[In the midst of this corruption] I nonetheless found consolation in seeing a great number of men and women who renounced all their possessions and left the world for the love of Christ: "Friars Minor" and "Sisters Minor." As for the brothers themselves, they live the life of the primitive Church of which it is written: "The whole group of believers was united, heart and soul." During the day they go into the cities and villages, giving themselves over to the active life of the apostolate; at night, they return to their hermitage or withdraw into solitude to live the contemplative life.

JACQUES DE VITRY

DAY 6
We Are Always in the Presence of God

Revel in God's holy name,
delight in seeking the Lord.
Look always for the power,
for the presence of God.

PSALM 105:3-4

MORNING READING

St. Francis felt like an exile, as long as he remained in this earthly life separated from God and, at the same time, his love of Christ had left him insensible to all earthly desires. Therefore, he tried to keep his spirit in the presence of God, by praying to him without intermission, so that he might not be without some comfort from his Beloved. Whether he was walking or sitting, at home or abroad, whether he was working or resting, he was so wholeheartedly intent on prayer that he seemed to have dedicated to it not only his heart and his soul, but all his efforts and all his time. He was often taken right out of himself in such an excess of devotion that he was lost in ecstasy. Then he experienced things which were beyond all human understanding, and he would be completely oblivious of all that went on about him.

ST. BONAVENTURE, *MINOR LIFE OF ST. FRANCIS*

For prayer and psalmody every hour is suitable, that while one's hands are busy with their tasks we may praise God with the tongue, or if not, with the heart.... Thus in the midst of our work we can fulfill the duty of prayer, giving thanks to him who has granted strength to our hands for performing our tasks, and cleverness to our minds for acquiring knowledge.... Thus we acquire a recollected spirit, when in every action we beg from God the success of our labors and satisfy our debt of gratitude to him ... and when we keep before our minds the aim of pleasing him.

ST. BASIL

FOR REFLECTION

Holy One, you are always present to us. We have only to remember that we move in your being, and lifting our hearts to you, we are at prayer. Every movement, every task, every thought, offered to you becomes prayer. Make me mindful of this as I move through my days. Your presence with me in all things is what can bind the many parts of my life into one, endless prayer.

EVENING READING

At all times and seasons, in every country and place, every day and all day, we must have a true and humble faith, and keep him in our hearts, where we must love, honor, adore, serve, praise and bless, glorify and acclaim, magnify and thank, the most high supreme and eternal God, Three and One, Father, Son, and Holy Spirit, Creator of all and Savior of those who believe in him, who hope in him, and who love him.

THE RULE OF 1221

When We Ask in Need, God Will Answer

Turn to God, be bright with joy;
you shall never be let down.
I begged and God heard,
took my burdens from me.

PSALM 34:6-7

MORNING READING

The saint, therefore, made it a point to keep himself in joy of heart and to preserve the unction of the Spirit and the *oil of gladness.* He avoided with the greatest care the miserable illness of dejection, so that if he felt it creeping over his mind even a little, he would have recourse very quickly to prayer. For he would say: "If the servant of God, as may happen, is disturbed in any way, he should rise immediately to pray and he should remain in the presence of the heavenly Father until he *restores unto him the joy of salvation.* For if he *remains stupefied* in sadness, the Babylonian stuff will increase, so that, unless it be at length driven out by tears, it will generate an abiding rust in the heart."

THOMAS OF CELANO, *THE SECOND LIFE OF ST. FRANCIS*

And he said to them, "Which of you who has a friend will go to him at midnight and say to him, 'Friend, lend me three loaves; for a friend of mine has arrived on a journey, and I have nothing to set before him'; and he will answer from within, 'Do not bother me; the door is now shut, and my children are with me in bed; I cannot get up and give you anything'? I tell you, though he will not get up and give him anything because he is his friend, yet because of his

importunity he will rise and give him whatever he needs. And I tell
you, Ask, and it will be given you; seek, and you will find; knock, and
it will be opened to you. For everyone who asks receives, and he who
seeks finds, and to him who knocks it will be opened."

LUKE 11:4-10

FOR REFLECTION

Holy One, help me to trust in your love and to persevere in prayer
even when I cannot sense the reply. You know me better than I do
myself. Open my spirit to receive the grace you send.

EVENING READING

In the course of one of his journeys, blessed Francis met the abbot
of a monastery who had much affection and veneration for him.
The abbot dismounted from his horse and talked with him for an
hour about the salvation of his soul; before leaving, he asked him
with great devotion to pray for him. "Gladly," he said. When the
abbot was some distance away, blessed Francis said to his
companion: "Brother, wait a few minutes: I want to pray for that
abbot as I promised I would." And he began to pray.

The abbot, however, continued on his way; he had not gone
very far when suddenly he received a visit of the Lord in his heart.
A sweet warmth came to his face and he was wrapped in ecstasy
for a brief moment. When he came to himself, he knew that
blessed Francis had prayed for him.

LEGEND OF PERUGIA

DAY 8

Prayer Opens Our Hearts to God's Provident Care

Bless the Lord each day
who carries our burden,
who keeps us alive,
our God who saves,
our escape from death.

PSALM 68:20-21

MORNING READING

We have left the world now and all we have to do is to be careful to obey God's will and please him. We must be very careful, or we will turn out to be like the earth by the wayside, or the stony or thorn-choked ground, as our Lord tells us in the Gospel....

We should beware especially of the malice and wiles of Satan; his only desire is to prevent man from raising his mind and heart to his Lord and God. He goes about, longing to steal man's heart away under the pretext of some good or useful interest, and obliterate the words and commandments of God from his memory. By the anxieties and worries of this life he tries to dull man's heart and make a dwelling for himself there. And so we must keep close watch over ourselves or we will be lost and turn our minds and hearts from God, because we think there is something worth having or doing, or that we will gain some advantage.

THE RULE OF 1221

Prayer is a vital necessity. Proof from the contrary is no less convincing: if we do not allow the Spirit to lead us, we fall back into the slavery of sin. How can the Holy Spirit be our life if our heart is far from him? (Nothing is equal to prayer; for what is impossible it makes possible, what is difficult, easy.... For it is impossible, utterly impossible, for the man who prays eagerly and invokes God ceaselessly ever to sin.)

CATECHISM OF THE CATHOLIC CHURCH

FOR REFLECTION

When our hearts are empty and long for God, the spirit of the world can fool us into seeking satisfaction in the distractions of the world.

O God Who Completes, turn me from the temptation to fill my emptiness with less than yourself. There is nothing I can do or have that is worth more than receiving you into my heart, opened wide through the gift of prayer.

EVENING READING

Prayer was his sure refuge in everything he did; he never relied on his own efforts, but put his trust in God's loving providence and cast the burden of his cares on him in insistent prayer. He was convinced that the grace of prayer was something a religious should long for above all else. No one, he declared, could make progress in God's service without it, and he used every means he could to make the friars concentrate on it.

ST. BONAVENTURE, MAJOR LIFE OF ST. FRANCIS

When We Flee, God Remains by Our Side

Where can I hide from you?
How can I escape your presence?
I scale the heavens, you are there!
I plunge to the depths, you are there!
If I fly toward the dawn,
or settle across the sea,
even there you take hold of me,
your right hand directs me.

PSALM 139:7-10

MORNING READING

So Francis still tried to flee the hand of God, and, forgetting for a while his paternal correction, he thought, amid the smiles of prosperity, of *the things of the world*; and, ignorant of the *counsel of God*, he still looked forward to accomplishing great deeds of worldly glory and vanity. For a certain nobleman of the city of Assisi was preparing himself in no mean way with military arms, and, puffed up by a gust of vainglory, vowed that he would go to Apulia to increase his wealth and fame. Upon hearing this, Francis, who was flighty and not a little rash, arranged to go with him; he was inferior to him in nobility of birth, but superior in generosity, poorer in the matter of wealth, but more lavish in giving things away.

THOMAS OF CELANO, *THE FIRST LIFE OF ST. FRANCIS*

I fled him, down the nights and down the days;
I fled him, down the arches of the years;
I fled him, down the labyrinthine ways
Of my own mind; and in the midst of tears
I hid from him, and under running laughter.
Up vistaed hopes, I sped;

And shot, precipitated,
Adown Titanic glooms of chasmed fears,
From those strong feet they followed, followed after.
But with unhurrying chase,
And unperturbed pace,
Deliberate speed, majestic instancy,
They beat—and a voice beat
More instant than the feet—
"All things betray thee, who betrayest me."

Francis Thompson

FOR REFLECTION

Many things tempt me to flee from God in my life. Sometimes it is fear of what will be demanded that drives me away. Yet, I will not know peace until I rest in you, Lord. You will not ask more than I can give. Imagine, the Creator of the universe is patiently calling to me without pause, until I turn and answer!

EVENING READING

He set out shortly afterwards but when he reached the next town, he heard God calling him by his first name as he lay asleep, and saying, "Francis, who can do more for you, a lord or his servant, a rich man or a beggar?" When he replied that a lord or a rich man could do more, he was asked, "Then why are you abandoning the Lord to devote yourself to a servant? Why are you choosing a beggar instead of God who is infinitely rich?" "Lord," replied Francis, "what will you have me do?" And God told him, "Go back to your own town. The vision which you saw foretold a spiritual achievement which will be accomplished in you by God's will, not man's." In the morning Francis went back to Assisi without delay. He was overjoyed and had no care for the future; he was already a model of obedience and he waited patiently on God's will.

St. Bonaventure, Major Life of St. Francis

Our Hearts Are Open to God's Grace

Stretch toward heaven, you gates,
open high and wide.
Let the glorious sovereign enter.
Who is this splendid ruler?
The Lord of power and might,
the conqueror of chaos.
Stretch toward heaven, you gates,
open high and wide.
Let the glorious sovereign enter.

PSALM 24:7-9

MORNING READING

Once Saint Francis spent a whole night in prayer saying nothing but: "O most holy Lord, I long to love thee. O most sweet Lord, I long to love thee." And while he was praying our Lord Jesus Christ appeared to him. Then Francis fell at his feet and said: "O my Lord, I have given thee my whole heart and body, and yet I desire with all my being to do more for thee if thou wilt but show me how."

A NEW FIORETTI

Thus was the spirituality of the saint of Assisi defined. His way of being was that of profound contemplation: contemplation viewed not as withdrawal from the world, but as entry into its deepest gift—the mystery of life, the presence of God in life and mirrored by life. He moved through life in contemplation, in a fundamental attitude of receptiveness to the Spirit and a primary attunement to the reality around him at all times. His manner of contemplation led to a deeply intentional life; the awareness of God's presence shaped how he lived every moment.

ST. FRANCIS AND THE FOOLISHNESS OF GOD

FOR REFLECTION

As the author of *The Cloud of Unknowing* says, prayer is simply a mindful openness to God with a desire to grow in goodness and surmount evil.

Ever-Present God, your son, Francis, moved through life with his spirit wide open to receive you in all moments and places. Help me throw open the gates of my heart to receive you no matter where I am, or what I am doing.

EVENING READING

The blessed father was accustomed not to pass over any visitation of the Spirit with negligence. When indeed such was offered, he followed it, and as long as the Lord would permit, he would enjoy the sweetness thus offered him. When, therefore, while he was pressed by some business or was intent upon a journey, he felt little by little certain touches of grace, he would taste the sweetest manna in frequent snatches. For also along the way, with his companions going on ahead, he would stand still, and turning the new inspiration to fruitfulness, he would not *receive the grace in vain.*

THOMAS OF CELANO, THE SECOND LIFE OF ST. FRANCIS

For God Alone

Poverty Is Treasure Hidden in the Field

I treasure your ways
more than great riches.

PSALM 119:14

MORNING READING

Among the supernatural gifts which Francis received from God, the Generous Giver, his love for absolute poverty constituted a special privilege which enabled him to grow rich in spiritual wealth. He saw that it had been the constant companion of the Son of God, but that now it was scorned by the whole world, and so he espoused it in undying love. For poverty's sake he abandoned his father and mother and divested himself of everything he had. No one was so greedy for gold as he was for poverty; no treasure was guarded as jealously as he guarded this Gospel pearl. From the first moment of his religious life until his death, his sole wealth consisted in a habit, a cord, and a pair of trousers, and he was content with that.

When the friars asked him privately what virtue made one dearest to Christ, he replied as if revealing his closest secret, "Believe me, my brothers, poverty is the special way of salvation. It is the source of humility and the root of all perfection and its fruit is manifold, though unseen. This is the treasure hidden in the field in the Gospel to buy which we must sell all—and anything that cannot be sold should be abandoned for love of it."

ST. BONAVENTURE, *MAJOR LIFE OF ST. FRANCIS*

Voluntarily poor one may be from philosophy or asceticism, for reasons of zeal, of charity, and others still. But Francis was poor from love. He made himself poor because his beloved Christ had been poor. He espoused Poverty because she had been "the inseparable companion of the Most High Son of God," and because for twelve centuries she has wandered about forsaken.

OMER ENGLEBERT

FOR REFLECTION

Jesus, fill my heart with love of you above all things. Grace me to see material goods not as ends in themselves, but as means of serving you and your people.

EVENING READING

At one time the vicar of the holy father, Peter of Cantania, seeing that St. Mary of the Portiuncula was visited by a great number of brothers from afar and that there were not sufficient alms to provide for their needs, said to St. Francis: "Brother, I do not know what I will do.... I do not have enough to provide for them properly. May it please you, I beg of you, that some of the goods of the entering novices be kept aside so that we might have recourse to them at the opportune time."

Francis said: "Strip the altar of the Blessed Virgin and take away its many ornaments, since you cannot otherwise come to the help of the needy. Believe me, she would be more pleased to have the Gospel of her son kept and her altar stripped than that the altar should be ornamented and her son despised."

THOMAS OF CELANO, *THE SECOND LIFE OF ST. FRANCIS*

DAY 12
Give Until It Hurts

Blest are those ready to help the poor;
in hard times God repays their care.

PSALM 41:2

MORNING READING

Another time, when Francis was returning from Siena, he met a certain poor man and said to his companion: "Brother, we must return this mantle to that poor man to whom it belongs. We borrowed it from him until we should meet someone poorer than ourselves." His companion, thinking about his father's need, obstinately refused, lest Francis provide for another by neglecting himself. The saint said to him: "I do not want to be a thief; for it would be considered a theft in us if we did not give to someone who is in greater need than we." The other gave in, and Francis gave over his mantle.

THOMAS OF CELANO, *THE SECOND LIFE OF ST. FRANCIS*

Jesus died on the Cross because that is what it took for him to do good to us—to save us from our selfishness in sin. He gave up everything to do the Father's will—to show us that we too must be willing to give up everything to do God's will—to love one another as he loves each of us. That is why we too must give to each other until it hurts.

It is not enough for us to say: "I love God," but I also have to love my neighbor. St. John says that you are a liar if you say you love God and you don't love your neighbor. How can you love God whom you do not see, if you do not love your neighbor whom you see, whom you touch, with whom you live? And so it is very important for us to realize that love, to be true, has to hurt. I must be willing to give whatever it takes not to harm other people and, in fact, to do good to them. This requires that I be willing to give until it hurts. Otherwise, there is no true love in me and I bring injustice, not peace, to those around me.

MOTHER TERESA

FOR REFLECTION

Jesus, giving from abundance is not difficult. Bless me with love that puts the needs of others before my own.

EVENING READING

We who lived with him testify to the greatness of his charity and compassion towards sick and healthy alike, both to his own friars and to other poor folk. For after persuading us not to be upset, he used to give away to the poor with great inward and outward joy even his own bodily necessities, which the friars had sometimes obtained with great trouble and difficulty, thus depriving himself even of things that he badly needed. Because of this the Minister General and his Guardian told him not to give away his habit to any friar without their permission. For in their devotion to him the friars used sometimes to ask him for his habit, and at once he would give it; but sometimes he divided it and gave away a portion, retaining part for himself, for he wore only a single habit.

MIRROR OF PERFECTION

We Are Always Beginners

Deep within me a voice says,
"Look for the face of God!"
So, I look for your face...
If my parents rejected me,
still God would take me in.

PSALM 27:8, 10

[Editor's note: After suffering a long illness in his youth, Francis began to turn his mind and heart toward God and God's call.]

MORNING READING

From that day on, therefore, he began to despise himself and to hold in some contempt the things he had admired and loved before. But not fully or truly, for he was not yet freed from the *cords of vanity* nor had he shaken off from his neck the yoke of evil servitude. It is indeed very hard to give up things one is accustomed to, and things that once enter into the mind are not easily eradicated; the mind, even though it has been kept away from them for a long time, returns to the things it once learned; and by constant repetition vice generally becomes second nature.

THOMAS OF CELANO, THE FIRST LIFE OF ST. FRANCIS

Just as I am, and waiting not
To rid my soul of one dark blot,
To thee, whose blood can cleanse each spot,
O Lamb of God, I come.
Just as I am, though tossed about
With many a conflict, many a doubt,

Fightings and fears within, without,
O Lamb of God, I come.

"THE LAMB OF GOD" BY CHARLOTTE ELLIOT
IN *THE BOOK OF HYMNS*

FOR REFLECTION

I am encouraged, Lord, by your acceptance of me as I am. Help me see today's opportunities to grow in faith and love.

EVENING READING

But, though the glorious father had been brought to the fulness of grace before God and shone among men of this world by his good works, he nevertheless thought always to begin more perfect works and, like the most skilled soldier in the *camps of God,* the enemy having been challenged, to stir up new wars. He proposed, under *Christ the prince,* to do great things, and, with his limbs failing and his body dying, he hoped for a victory over the enemy in a new struggle. For true virtue knows not a limit of time, since the expectation of a reward is eternal. Therefore he was afire with a very great desire to return to the first beginnings of humility and, by reason of the immensity of his love, *rejoicing in hope,* he thought to recall his body to its former subjection, even though it had already come to such an extremity....

Though he found it necessary to moderate his early rigor because of his infirmity, he would still say: "Let us begin, brothers, to serve the Lord God, for up to now we have made little or no progress." He did not consider that he had laid hold of his goal as yet, and persevering untiringly in his purpose of attaining holy *newness of life,* he hoped always to make a beginning.

THOMAS OF CELANO, *THE FIRST LIFE OF ST. FRANCIS*

We Are What God Made Us

You created every part of me,
knitting me in my mother's womb.
You saw my body grow
according to your design.

PSALM 139:13, 16

MORNING READING

He also chose this foundation of perfect humility and poverty for himself. Even though he was an exalted person in the Church of God, of his own free will he wanted to be regarded as being on the lowest rung not only in the Church but even among his brothers.

One day when he was preaching to the people of Terni in the town square in front of the bishop's palace, the bishop of the city, a discerning and spiritual man, listened to the sermon. When it was over, he rose and among other words of exhortation said: "From the time he planted and built his Church, the Lord has always endowed her with holy persons to make her grow by word and example. And in these latter days, he has shed luster on her through this poor, humble, and unlettered man. (As he said this, he pointed his finger toward Francis.) That is why you are bound to love and honor the Lord and to keep yourselves from all sin, for he has not bestowed such great favor on all nations."

Then the bishop came down from the place where he had spoken to the people and entered his cathedral with blessed Francis. Then blessed Francis bowed before the lord bishop, threw himself at his feet and said to him: "In truth, lord bishop, I say to you: no man in this world has ever paid me the honor you have today. Other men say: He is a saint! Thereby they attributed glory and holiness to a creature and not to the Creator. You, on the contrary, as a discerning man, have made a distinction between what is base and what is precious."

LEGEND OF PERUGIA

Do not wish to be anything but what you are, and try to be that perfectly.

ST. FRANCIS DE SALES

FOR REFLECTION

Father, help me to discover and rejoice in my true identity, and be faithful to that above all else.

EVENING READING

Blessed the religious who takes no more pride in the good that God says and does through him, than in that which he says and does through someone else. It is wrong for anyone to be anxious to receive more from his neighbor than he himself is willing to give to God.

Blessed the religious who has no more regard for himself when people praise him and make much of him than when they despise and revile him and say that he is ignorant. What a man is before God, that he is and no more.

THE ADMONITIONS

We Keep Ourselves in the Dust of Humility

Keep my pride in check,
break its grip;
I shall be free of blame
for deadly sin.

PSALM 19:14

MORNING READING

When he was acclaimed as a saint by the crowds, he would say, "I might have sons and daughters yet. Don't praise me as if I were safe. You should never praise anyone until you see how he turned out in the end." That is what he said to others and then, addressing himself, he would add, "If almighty God had done so much for a criminal, he would be more thankful than you, Francis." He used to often tell the friars, "No one should flatter himself for anything a sinner is capable of doing. A sinner can fast, pray, weep, and do physical penance. The one thing he cannot do is to remain faithful to God. Anyone who gives back to God the praise which belongs to him really has something to boast about, if he serves him faithfully and attributes to him the gifts he bestows."

SAINT BONAVENTURE, MAJOR LIFE OF ST. FRANCIS

At first you might say, "I am; I see and feel that I am. And not only do I exist but I possess all sorts of personal talents and gifts." But after counting up all these in your mind, you could still go a step farther and draw them all together in a single all-embracing prayer such as this:

That which I am and the way that I am,
with all my gifts of nature and grace,
you have given to me, O Lord, and you are
all this. I offer it all to you, principally
to praise you and to help my fellow Christians
and myself.

THE BOOK OF PRIVY COUNSELING

FOR REFLECTION

Creator, help me remember that my gifts are from you. When I do well, I offer thanksgiving to you. When I misuse what I have been given, I ask for forgiveness.

EVENING READING

The Blessed Francis was so much honored for his holiness by the people that they used not only to kiss his hands, but even his feet. He, however, seemed in no way put out by such reverence; but his companions were horrified. "Brother," said one of them to him, "are you aware of what is happening? Do you not see what you are doing? The people are worshipping you, and yet you don't attempt to stop them, but seem rather to rejoice in it!" ...

Then Francis said to him: "Look, brother; all this reverence which is paid to me I never take to myself, but I simply pass it all on to God. And as for me, I keep myself in the dust of humility and all honor I give to God. Thus the people benefit, for it is God whom they are worshipping, though they see him only in his creatures."

A NEW FIORETTI

When We Need God, Nothing Else Suffices

Why are you sad, my heart?
Why do you grieve?
Wait for the Lord.
I will yet praise God my savior.

PSALM 42:12

MORNING READING

For, indeed, while this man was still in the glow of youthful passion, and the age of wantonness was urging him on immoderately to fulfill the demands of youth; and while, not knowing how to restrain himself, he was stirred by the venom of the serpent of old, suddenly the divine vengeance, or, perhaps better, the divine unction, came upon him and sought first to recall his erring senses by visiting upon him mental distress and bodily suffering, according to the saying of the prophet: *Behold I will hedge up thy way with thorns, and I will stop it up with a wall.* Thus, worn down by a long illness, as man's stubbornness deserves when it can hardly be corrected except by punishments, he began to think of things other than he was used to thinking upon. When he had recovered somewhat and had begun to walk about the house with the support of a cane to speed the recovery of his health, he went outside one day and began to look about at the surrounding landscape with great interest. But the beauty of the fields, the pleasantness of the vineyards, and whatever else was beautiful to look upon, could stir in him no delight. He wondered therefore at the sudden change that had come over him, and those who took delight in such things he considered very foolish.

THOMAS OF CELANO, *THE FIRST LIFE OF ST. FRANCIS*

He also said, "Do not give your heart to that which does not satisfy your heart."

ABBA POEMEN

FOR REFLECTION

In the midst of plenty, my soul is restless, Lord. Enlighten me with the knowledge that you alone can fill the empty places in my heart. Give me the desire for you alone.

[Editor's note: One night on his way to Apulia to earn honor in battle, Francis had a vision of his home filled with armor and trappings of war.]

EVENING READING

When he awoke, he arose in the morning with a glad heart, and considering the vision an omen of great success, he felt sure that his journey to Apulia would come out well. *He did not know what to say* and he did not as yet recognize the task given him from heaven. Nevertheless, he might have understood that his interpretation of the vision was not correct, for while the vision bore some resemblance to things pertaining to war, his heart was not filled with his usual happiness over such things. He had to use some force on himself to carry out his designs and to complete the proposed journey.

THOMAS OF CELANO, THE FIRST LIFE OF ST. FRANCIS

Pilgrims, We Leave Concerns of the World Behind Us

Your temple is my joy,
Lord of heaven's might.
I am eager for it,
eager for the courts of God.
One day within your courts
is worth a thousand without.

PSALM 84:2-3, 11

MORNING READING

"Anyone who wants to practice perfect poverty," he said, "must renounce all worldly wisdom and even secular learning, to a certain extent. Divested of these possessions, he will be able to make the great acts of God his theme (cf. Ps 73, 15-16) and offer himself naked to the embrace of the Crucified. Anyone who clings to his own opinions in the depths of his heart has not renounced the world perfectly."

When speaking about poverty to the friars, Francis often quoted the words of the Gospel, "Foxes have holes, and the birds of the air their resting-places; the Son of Man has nowhere to lay his head" (Mt 8:20), and he gave orders that the houses they built should be small, like those of the poor. There the friars should live not as if the house belonged to them, but as strangers and pilgrims in a house which was not their own. It was part of a pilgrim's life, he said, to shelter under another's roof and pass on peacefully, longing for home.

ST. BONAVENTURE, *MAJOR LIFE OF ST. FRANCIS*

Just as true pilgrims going to Jerusalem leave behind house and land, wife and children, making themselves poor and bereft of all possessions in order to travel lightly the whole way, so, if you would be a spiritual pilgrim, you must divest yourself of all that you possess, good deeds and bad, and cast them all behind you; you must become so poor in your own estimation that there is nothing of your own doing that you can rely on: just desire ever more grace and love, and seek always the spiritual presence of Jesus. If you do this, then you will set your heart fully on getting to Jerusalem and nowhere else but there. This means that you will set your heart entirely on having nothing but the love of Jesus, and the spiritual sighting of him that he will give you; that alone is what you have been created and redeemed for, and that is your beginning and your end, your joy and your bliss.

WALTER HILTON

FOR REFLECTION

God, my destination, help me remember that I am a pilgrim in this world, making my way to eternal life with you.

EVENING READING

We should have no more use or regard for money in any of its forms than for dust. Those who think it is worth more or who are greedy for it, expose themselves to the danger of being deceived by the devil. We have left everything we had behind us; we must be very careful now not to lose the kingdom of heaven for so little.

THE RULE OF 1221

Detachment Gives Us Freedom

Guide me along your path,
a way of delight.
Open my heart to your laws
and not to riches.
Your law is better
than untold wealth.

PSALM 119:35-36, 72

MORNING READING

Poverty, which was all they had to meet their expenses, made them ready to undertake any task, while giving them strength for any kind of toil and leaving them free to travel without difficulty. They possessed nothing that belonged to this world; they loved nothing, and so they feared to lose nothing. They were free from care, with no anxiety to disturb them or worry to distract them. Their hearts were at peace as they lived from day to day, looking forward to the morrow without a thought as to where they would find shelter for the night. Their very poverty seemed to them overflowing abundance as, in the words of the prophet, they "made much of the little they had" (cf. Sir 29, 30).

ST. BONAVENTURE, *MAJOR LIFE OF ST. FRANCIS*

Oh, how peace comes flooding into the soul, when once it learns to rise above its natural sensitiveness! To be really poor in spirit—there's no joy like it. You ask, with complete unconcern, for something you really need, and the other person not only refuses, but wants you to hand over something you've got already; what do you do? Why, what our Lord advises us to do: "If a man is ready to go to the law with thee over thy coat, let him have it and thy cloak with it." I suppose the idea of giving up one's cloak is renouncing the last shred of dignity, treating oneself as everybody's drudge, everybody's slave. Well, now that you've taken off your coat, you're in a good position for walking—running if you want to.

ST. THÉRESE OF LISIEUX

FOR REFLECTION

Lord, grant me grace to drop the burden of excess like the discarded cloak in Scripture. Then I can be free to greet each day with an uncluttered spirit, free to meet you there.

EVENING READING

The brothers often asked the advice of the Bishop, who received Francis with kindness, but said: "It seems to me that it is very hard and difficult to possess nothing in the world." To this the blessed Francis replied: "My Lord, if we had any possessions we should also be forced to have arms to protect them, since possessions are a cause of disputes and strife, and in many ways we should be hindered from loving God and our neighbor. Therefore in this life we wish to have no temporal possessions."

LEGEND OF THE THREE COMPANIONS

Work of God

We Are Ministers of Compassion and Love

For love of family and friends
I say, "Peace be with you!"
For love of the Lord's own house
I pray for your good.

PSALM 122:8-9

[Editor's note: Francis described some of the qualities the leader of his order should possess.]

MORNING READING

He should give devout comfort to those in trouble, for he is the ultimate resort of the distressed; for if they cannot obtain healing remedies from him, the disease of despair will overpower the afflicted. He should show mildness in order to bend the unruly to gentleness, and forego some of his own rights if it will win a soul. He should show pity to those who desert the Order, as to sheep who have perished, and never refuse mercy to them, realizing that temptations that could drive them to such a fall must have been overwhelming, and that were God to permit him to be tested in the same way, he might himself fall into an even deeper pit.

MIRROR OF PERFECTION

"And it cannot be otherwise, because love of me and of her neighbor are one and the same thing, and, so far as the soul loves me, she loves her neighbor, because love towards him issues from me.... I could easi-ly have created men possessed of all that they should need both for body and soul, but I wish that one should have need of the other, and that they should be my ministers to administer the graces and the gifts

that they have received from me.... I have made men my ministers,
and placed them in diverse stations and various ranks, in order that
they may make use of the virtue of love."

St. Catherine of Siena

FOR REFLECTION

Loving God, you depend on me to do your work. Open my eyes
to the needs of others.

EVENING READING

On another occasion, while blessed Francis was living in the same
place, one of the friars, who was a spiritual man and an early mem-
ber of the Order, was ill and very weak. As he looked at him, the
holy Father felt great compassion for him. But because at that
time the friars, both healthy and sick, were cheerfully regarding
their poverty as plenty, and would not use or ask for medicines in
sickness, but willingly accepted bodily privations, blessed Francis
said to himself, "If only this brother could eat some ripe grapes
first thing in the morning, I think they would do him good."

And he acted on this idea, for he rose very early one day, and
calling the friar to him privately, led him into a vineyard near the
friary. Choosing a vine where the grapes were good to eat, he sat
down beside the vine with the friar, and began to eat the grapes
lest the brother should be ashamed to eat alone. And as they ate
the friar was cured, and they praised God together. This friar
remembered the compassion and kindness of the most holy Father
for the rest of his life, and often used to tell the brethren about it
with devotion and tears.

Mirror of Perfection

God Is Always Ready to Forgive

The Lord is tender and caring,
slow to anger, rich in love.
God will not accuse us long,
nor bring our sins to trial,
nor exact from us in kind
what our sins deserve.

PSALM 103:8-10

MORNING READING

These are the wretched circumstances among which the man whom we venerate today as a saint, for he is truly a saint, lived in his youth; and almost up to the twenty-fifth year of his age, he squandered and wasted his time miserably. Indeed, he outdid all his contemporaries in vanities and he came to be a promoter of evil and was more abundantly zealous for all kinds of foolishness. He was the admiration of all and strove to outdo the rest in the pomp of vainglory. On the other hand, he was a very kindly person, easy and affable, even making himself foolish because of it; for because of these qualities many ran after him, doers of evil and promoters of crime. And thus overwhelmed by a host of evil companions, proud and high-minded, he walked about the streets of Babylon until the *Lord looked down from heaven* and for his own name's sake removed his *wrath far off* and for his praise bridled Francis lest he should perish. *The hand of the Lord* therefore came *upon him* and a change was wrought by the right hand of the Most High, that through him an assurance might be granted to sinners that they had been restored to grace and that he might become an example to all of conversion to God.

THOMAS OF CELANO, *THE FIRST LIFE OF ST. FRANCIS*

As Jesus passed on from there, he saw a man called Matthew sitting at the tax office; and he said to him, "Follow me." And he rose and followed him.

And as he sat at table in the house, behold, many tax collectors and sinners came and sat down with Jesus and his disciples. And when the Pharisees saw this, they said to his disciples, "Why does your teacher eat with tax collectors and sinners?" But when he heard it, he said, "Those who are well have no need of a physician, but those who are sick. Go and learn what this means, 'I desire mercy, and not sacrifice.' For I came not to call the righteous, but sinners."

MATTHEW 9:9-13

FOR REFLECTION

Lord Jesus, recognizing my own sin, and emboldened by the love you showed to Francis, I ask for your mercy.

EVENING READING

I should like you to prove that you love God and me, his servant and yours, in the following way. There should be no friar in the whole world who has fallen into sin, no matter how far he has fallen, who will ever fail to find your forgiveness for the asking, if he will only look into your eyes. And if he does not ask forgiveness, you should ask him if he wants it. And should he appear before you again a thousand times, you should love him more than you love me, so that you may draw him to God; you should always have pity on such friars.

LETTER TO A MINISTER

Ordinary Work Can Be the Work of God

God, teach me your ways
and I will follow them closely.
Help me understand your will,
that I may cherish your law.

PSALM 119:33-34

MORNING READING

On one occasion he fell victim to a serious doubt; and some time afterwards, when he returned from where he had been praying, he put it before the friars who were closest to him, to have it resolved. "What do you think of this, Brothers?" he said. "Which do you think is better? That I should devote all my time to prayer, or that I should go about preaching? I am a poor and worthless religious. I have no education and I am inexperienced in speaking; I have received the gift of prayer rather than that of preaching. Besides, prayer earns merit and a multitude of special favors, while preaching seems to be only a way of sharing the gifts which have been received from heaven. Prayer helps to purify the desires of the heart and unites a person to the one, true, and supreme Good, while giving an increase of virtue. The labor of preaching allows dust to enter into the soul and involves a lot of distraction and relaxation of religious discipline. In prayer we talk to God and listen to him and live a life worthy of the angels, with the angels for our companions. When preaching, we have to descend to the level of human beings and live among them as one of them, thinking and seeing and hearing and speaking about human affairs. But, on the other hand, there is one argument which seems to count more than all the rest in God's eyes and it is this: the only-begotten Son of God, who is Wisdom itself, came down from the Father's embrace to save souls. He wanted to teach the world by his own example and bring a message of salvation to the men whom he had redeemed at the price of his Precious Blood, washing them clean in it and upholding them by its taste. He kept nothing for himself, but generously surrendered all for our salvation."

ST. BONAVENTURE, *MAJOR LIFE OF ST. FRANCIS*

Work, even the most simple, performed with constant perfection in the midst of inevitable difficulties, spells heroism.

POPE BENEDICT XV

FOR REFLECTION

Jesus, help me see my life and work with all its distractions as an opportunity to do your work in the world.

[Editor's note: Francis sought the help of Brother Silvester and St. Clare in discerning how God would have him use his gifts.]

EVENING READING

He now chose two of the friars and sent them to Brother Silvester. They were to tell him to ask God to solve his doubts and send him the answer in God's name. He sent the same message to St. Clare, telling her to pray with her sisters and find out God's will by means of the holiest and most simple of the sisters who lived under her. By the inspiration of the Holy Spirit, Brothers Silvester and St. Clare both came to the same conclusion. It was God's will that Francis should go out to preach as a herald of Christ.

ST. BONAVENTURE, *MAJOR LIFE OF ST. FRANCIS*

We Should Use Time Wisely

Trust God and do good,
settle down and be at peace.
Give your life to the Lord.

PSALM 37:3

MORNING READING

From the time that this man began to cling to the Lord, having put aside all transitory things, he allowed hardly a moment of time to pass unused. Indeed, though he had already laid up an abundance of merits in the *treasure house* of the Lord, he was always ready, always zealous for spiritual exercises. Not to do something good he considered a grave offense; not to advance he judged to be a falling back. Once when he was staying in a cell at Siena, he called his sleeping companions one night, saying: "I have asked the Lord, brothers, to deign to show me when I am his servant. And the most kind Lord just now deigned to give me this reply: 'Know that you are then truly my servant when you think, speak, and do holy things.' Therefore have I called you, brothers, because I wish to be filled with shame before you if at any time I do nothing of these three things."

THOMAS OF CELANO, *THE SECOND LIFE OF ST. FRANCIS*

And the Lord, seeking his own laborer in the multitude of the people to whom he addresses the foregoing admonitions, says again: "Who is the man that loves life, who desires length of days" in order to enjoy good things? Shouldst thou, hearing this, make answer, "I am he," God says to thee, "if thou wilt have true and everlasting life, keep thy tongue from evil and thy lips from words of deceit. Forsake evil and do good; seek after peace and pursue it." And when you shall have done these things, mine eyes shall be upon you and mine ears shall be open to your prayers. And before you shall call upon me, I will say, "Lo, here I am."

THE RULE OF ST. BENEDICT

FOR REFLECTION

Time is God's gift. Whether at work, play, or rest, I offer the minutes to you, Lord. Let me not waste them, but use them well, giving you glory.

EVENING READING

The friars who have a trade should work at it, provided that it is no obstacle to their spiritual progress and can be practised without scandal. The Psalmist tells us, *You shall eat the fruit of your handiwork; happy shall you be, and favoured* (127:2); and St. Paul adds, *If any man will not work, neither let him eat* (2 Thes 3:10). Everyone should remain at the trade and in the position in which he was called. They are allowed to have the tools which they need for their trade.

All the friars must work hard doing good, as it has been said, "Always be doing something worthwhile; then the devil will always find you busy," and "Idleness is the enemy of the soul." And so those who serve God should be always busy praying or doing good.

THE RULE OF 1221

DAY 23
The Good We Do Is the Spirit at Work

All his glory is in your victory,
for you invest him with royal splendor,
confer on him lasting blessings,
and give him joy in your presence.
The king relies on the Most High,
God's love becomes his strength.

PSALM 21:6-8

MORNING READING

Christ, the power of God, Christ the wisdom of God (1 Cor 1 24), whom the Spirit of God had anointed, was with his servant Francis in everything he did, lending him eloquence in preaching sound doctrine and glorifying him by the extraordinary power of his miracles. Francis' words were like a blazing fire which penetrated the depths of the heart and filled the minds of his hearers with wonder. They had no claim to any literary style, but gave every sign of being the result of divine inspiration.

He was due to preach before the pope and the cardinals on one occasion and at the suggestion of the bishop of Ostia he learned a carefully prepared sermon by heart. But when he stood before them all to deliver his edifying message, his mind went blank and he could not remember a word. He told them what had happened quite humbly and invoked the aid of the Holy Spirit. Then his tongue was suddenly unloosed and he spoke so eloquently that he moved the hearts of his exalted listeners to true sorrow, and it was clear that it was the Spirit of God who spoke, not he.

ST. BONAVENTURE, *MAJOR LIFE OF ST. FRANCIS*

When I came to you, brethren, I did not come proclaiming to you the testimony of God in lofty words or wisdom. For I decided to know nothing among you except Jesus Christ and him crucified. And I was with you in weakness and in much fear and trembling; and my speech and my message were not in plausible words of wisdom, but in demonstration of the Spirit and power, that your faith might not rest in the wisdom of men but in the power of God....

Now we have received not the spirit of the world, but the Spirit which is from God, that we might understand the gifts bestowed on us by God. And we impart this in words not taught by human wisdom, but taught by the Spirit, interpreting spiritual truths to those who possess the Spirit.

1 CORINTHIANS 2:1-7, 10-13

FOR REFLECTION

Source of Wisdom, open me to your Spirit. Fill me so I can do your work in the world.

EVENING READING

He also said: "An artist who paints our Lord or the Blessed Virgin honors them and recalls them to our mind; nevertheless, the painting claims no other merit than what it is, a creation made of wood and color. God's servant is like a painting: a creature of God, through whom God is honored because of his blessings. He must not lay claim to any more merit than the wood and color do. Honor and glory must be given to God alone."

LEGEND OF PERUGIA

DAY 24
We Proclaim God's Word Without Fear

I would speak your word to kings,
and not be ashamed.

PSALM 119:46

[Editor's note: Desiring to convert the Muslims, and longing for martyrdom, Francis took a companion and journeyed to Syria.]

MORNING READING

When they had gone farther, they were met by men of the sultan's army, who fell upon them like wolves upon sheep and seized them fiercely. Then, exhausted as they were by the ill-treatment they had received, they were dragged before the sultan by God's providence, just as Francis wished. The sultan asked them by whom and why and in what capacity they had been sent, and how they got there; but Francis replied intrepidly that they had been sent by God, not by man, to show him and his subjects the way of salvation and proclaim the truth of the Gospel message. He proclaimed the triune God and Jesus Christ, the Savior of all, with such steadfastness, with such courage and spirit, that it was clear the promise of the Gospel had been fulfilled in him, "I will give you such eloquence and such wisdom as all your adversaries shall not be able to withstand, or to confute" (Lk 21:15).

When the sultan saw his enthusiasm and courage, he listened to him willingly and pressed him to stay with him. Then he offered Francis a number of valuable presents, but the saint was anxious only for the salvation of souls. The sultan was lost in admiration at the sight of such perfect disregard for worldly wealth and he felt greater respect than ever for the saint.

ST. BONAVENTURE, *MAJOR LIFE OF ST. FRANCIS*

God always gives his grace abundantly; they are free to accept or reject the faith.... Our task is to be the successors to the first apostles and evangelists. The word is mighty, but example, love and prayer are a thousand times more so. We must give them the example of a perfect life, of a higher and holy life; we must love them with the all powerful love that draws love; we must pray for them with hearts warm enough to bring down upon them a superabundance of divine grace. Then we cannot fail to convert them.

BROTHER CHARLES DE FOUCAULD

FOR REFLECTION

Jesus, you fearlessly announced the Good News by word and example. Help me live always according to your teachings. When my faith contradicts current values, give me courage to speak and act in ways that proclaim your truth.

EVENING READING

Francis had first convinced himself of the truth of what he preached to others by practicing it in his own life and so he proclaimed the truth confidently, without fear of reproof. He denounced evil wherever he found it, and made no effort to palliate it; from him a life of sin met with outspoken rebuke, not support. He spoke with equal candor to great and small and he was just as happy addressing a handful of listeners as a large gathering.

ST. BONAVENTURE, *MAJOR LIFE OF ST. FRANCIS*

We Are Not to Be Deaf Hearers
of the Gospel

I never forget your word,
for it is my life.
I am yours, save me!

PSALM 119:93

MORNING READING

As he was living there by the Church of Our Lady, Francis prayed to her who had conceived the Word, full of grace and truth, begging her insistently and with tears to become his Advocate. Then he was granted the true spirit of the Gospel by the intercession of the Mother of Mercy and he brought it to fruition. He was at Mass one day on the feast of one of the apostles and the passage of the Gospel where our Lord sends out his disciples to preach and tells them how they are to live according to the Gospel was read. When Francis heard that they were not to provide gold or silver or copper to fill their purses, that they were not to have a wallet for the journey or a second coat, no shoes or staff, he was overjoyed. He grasped the meaning of the passage immediately in his love for apostolic poverty and committed it to memory. "This is what I want," he exclaimed. "This is what I long for with all my heart." There and then he took off his shoes and laid aside his staff. He conceived a horror of money or wealth of any kind and he wore only one tunic, changing his leather belt for a rope. The whole desire of his heart was to put what he had heard into practice and conform to the rule of life given to the Apostles in everything.

ST. BONAVENTURE, MAJOR LIFE OF ST. FRANCIS

We all talk about the little way, and mothers especially know how one meal follows on another, and daily there is washing, and the house to pick up, and the wild romantic glamour of married life soon fades to give place to something deeper. It is the same with the work. People come in all of a glow to help the poor, and their compassion makes them think there must be some quicker way to serve them.... But the immediate work remains, the works of mercy, and there are few to do them. Perseverance, endurance, faithfulness to the poor—we should be wedded to Lady Poverty as St. Francis was—these are the things to stress.

DOROTHY DAY

FOR REFLECTION

Jesus, sometimes I think my life is insignificant and makes no difference in the redemption of this world. Yet, through Scripture you call to me. Open my ears to your voice. Open my heart to respond.

[Editor's note: After hearing the Gospel read at Mass, Francis was inspired to follow it as literally as possible.]

EVENING READING

He designed for himself a tunic that bore a likeness to the cross, that by means of it he might beat off all temptations of the devil; he designed a very rough tunic so that by it he might crucify the flesh with all its vices and sins; he designed a very poor and mean tunic, one that would not excite the covetousness of the world. The other things that he had heard, however, he longed with the greatest diligence and the greatest reverence to perform. For he was not a deaf hearer of the Gospel, but committing all that he had heard to praiseworthy memory, he tried diligently to carry it out to the letter.

THOMAS OF CELANO, THE FIRST LIFE OF ST. FRANCIS

DAY 26
Knowledge of Scripture
Directs Our Actions

How do the young stay pure?
By staying close to your word!
I seek you with all my heart.
Do not let me stray!

PSALM 119:9-10

MORNING READING

St. Francis had never studied Sacred Scripture, but unwearied application to prayer and the continual practice of virtue had purified his spiritual vision, so that his keen intellect was bathed in the radiance of eternal light and penetrated its depths. Free from every stain ... by affective love he entered where theologians with their science stand outside. Once he had read something in the sacred books and understood its meaning, he impressed it indelibly on his memory; anything he had once grasped carefully, he meditated upon continually.

When the friars asked him if he would allow the learned men who were entering the Order to continue the study of Sacred Scripture, he replied, "I do not mind, provided that they do not neglect prayer, after the example of Christ of whom we are told that he prayed more than he studied. They should not study merely in order to have something to say; they should study so as to practice what they have learned and then encourage others to do likewise."

ST. BONAVENTURE, MAJOR LIFE OF ST. FRANCIS

O most merciful Redeemer, friend and brother, may we know you more clearly, love you more dearly, and follow you more nearly, for your own sake.

St. Richard of Chichester

FOR REFLECTION

Lord Jesus, fill me with longing to immerse myself in your Word. Help me to read Scripture prayerfully, with the expectation of being led deeper into the knowledge and love of God. As I experience your presence in those sacred writings, increase my desire to follow your way.

EVENING READING

St. Paul tells us, *The letter kills, but the spirit gives life* (2 Cor 3:6). A man has been killed by the letter when he wants to know quotations only so that people will think he is very learned and he can make money to give to his relatives and friends. A religious has been killed by the letter when he has no desire to follow the spirit of Sacred Scripture, but wants to know what it says only so that he can explain it to others. On the other hand, those have received life from the spirit of Sacred Scripture who, by their words and example, refer to the most high God, to whom belongs all good, all that they know or wish to know, and do not allow their knowledge to become a source of self-complacency.

The Admonitions

Take Up Your Cross

In Fear, I Call Upon the Lord

From the depths I call to you,
Lord, hear my cry.
If you record our sins,
Lord, who could survive?
But because you forgive
we stand in awe.

PSALM 130:1-4

[Editor's note: Learning his son, Francis, was staying in an old church, Pietro Bernardone gathered friends and neighbors and went to find him.]

MORNING READING

But he, the new athlete of Christ, when he heard of the threats of those who were pursuing him and when he got knowledge of their coming, wanting to *give place to wrath*, hid himself in a certain secret pit which he himself had prepared for just such an emergency. The pit that was in that house was known probably to one person alone; in it he hid so continuously for one month that he hardly dared leave it to provide for his human needs. Food, when it was given to him, he ate in the secrecy of the pit, and every service was rendered to him by stealth. Praying, he prayed always with a torrent of tears that the Lord would deliver him from the hands of those who were persecuting his soul, and that he would fulfill his pious wishes in his loving kindness; *in fasting and in weeping* he begged for the clemency of the Savior, and, distrusting his own efforts, he *cast* his whole *care upon the Lord*.

THOMAS OF CELANO, *THE FIRST LIFE OF ST. FRANCIS*

There is an ancient monastic concept known as compunction. The word itself carries all sorts of resonances. It is the experience of being touched or pierced (punctio) *by the awareness of my true state before God, so at its heart lies a sense of pain, of stinging, a sensation of being pricked. It means also that I am stung into action, aroused from torpor and complacency, and now long to do better. Here is something positive, feeling God's love drawing me on to better things, calling me to a new future. I am touched, overwhelmed by the love of a God who forgives me and in the face of that love I long for compromise to cease and instead to respond totally to this amazing love which forgives and frees. While I am being forced to face ultimate truths about myself I am also at the same time being brought face to face with a loving trust in the God who saves.*

ESTHER DE WAAL

FOR REFLECTION

Lord God, like Francis I am afraid. Give me courage to go into the world trusting that, broken and worthless as I am, you love me and have work for me to do.

EVENING READING

While he was living in the friary of S. Mary, a very grave temptation was inflicted on him for the good of his soul. He was so tormented in mind and body by this, that he often withdrew from the company of the friars because he could not show them his usual cheerfulness. Nevertheless, he continued to discipline himself by abstinence from food, drink, and speech; and he prayed more constantly and shed more abundant tears, so that the Lord might be pleased to grant some remedy strong enough for so great a trial.

MIRROR OF PERFECTION

When We Are Lost in Darkness, God Will Be Our Light

God, your people seek shelter,
safe in the warmth of your wings.
They feast at your full table,
slake their thirst in your cool stream,
for you are the fount of life,
you give us light and we see.

PSALM 36:8-10

MORNING READING

At another time when he was walking near Padua with a companion, while on a missionary journey from Lombardy to the Marches of Treviso, they were overtaken by nightfall and enveloped in pitch darkness. The road was dangerous in the dark because of the river and the marshes and his companion said to him, "Father, pray that we may be kept safe from all danger." The saint replied confidently, "God has power to banish the darkness and give us light, if it pleases him in his kindness." The words were scarcely out of his mouth when a brilliant light shone about them with a heavenly radiance and they could see their way clearly and for quite a distance around, although it was dark everywhere else. By its guidance they found their way and were comforted in spirit. They still had a long way to go until they arrived where they were to spend the night, but they finished their journey safely, singing hymns of praise to God.

ST. BONAVENTURE, *MAJOR LIFE OF ST. FRANCIS*

Lead, kindly Light, amid the encircling gloom,
  Lead thou me on;
The night is dark, and I am far from home,
  Lead thou me on.
Keep thou my feet; I do not ask to see
The distant scene; one step enough for me.

So long thy power hath blessed me, sure it still
  Will lead me on,
O'er moor and fen, o'er crag and torrent, till
  The night is gone....

JOHN HENRY NEWMAN
"LEAD KINDLY LIGHT"

FOR REFLECTION

O First Light, who dispelled empty darkness with spinning galaxies and shining suns, enter into my own darkness of spirit. Scatter fear and trembling with your luminous presence.

EVENING READING

He embraced all things with a rapture of unheard-of devotion, speaking to them of the Lord and admonishing them to praise him. He spared lights, lamps, and candles, not wishing to extinguish their brightness with his hand, for he regarded them as a symbol of Eternal Light.

THOMAS OF CELANO, *THE SECOND LIFE OF ST. FRANCIS*

We Are Called to Take Up Our Cross

My people, if you would only listen!
Israel, walk in my ways!

PSALM 81:14

[Editor's note: After embracing the leper on the road, Francis con-
tinued to grow in God's grace. He sought time to be alone and pray.]

MORNING READING

After that he began to frequent secluded spots where he could
mourn for his sins, and there as he poured out his whole soul with
groans beyond all utterance, he was eventually found worthy to be
heard by God, after long and importunate prayer. One day as he
prayed in one of his usual haunts, he became completely absorbed
in God in the excess of his fervor. Then Jesus Christ appeared to
him, hanging on his cross. His soul melted at the sight and the
memory of Christ's passion was impressed on the depths of his
heart so vividly that whenever he thought of it, he could scarcely
restrain his sighs and tears, as he afterwards confessed towards the
end of his life. He realized immediately that the words of the
Gospel were addressed to him, "If you have a mind to come my
way, renounce yourself, and take up your cross and follow me" (cf.
Mt 16: 24).

ST. BONAVENTURE, *MAJOR LIFE OF ST. FRANCIS*

Go I this day according to thy laws, O God,
Pass I this day as pass the saints in heaven.

Thou loving Christ who wast hanged upon the tree,
Each day and each night remember I thy covenant;
In my lying down and rising up I yield me to thy cross,
In my life and my death my health thou art and my peace.

THE CELTIC VISION

FOR REFLECTION

Jesus, being totally faithful to your mission led you to the cross. Give me faith and courage to follow your example, and to respond faithfully to God's call in my own life, no matter the cost.

EVENING READING

With his companions Francis now went to live in an abandoned hut near Assisi, where they lived from hand to mouth according to the rule of poverty, in toil and penury, drawing their strength rather from tears of compunction than from any bodily food. They spent the time praying continuously, devoting themselves especially to fervent mental prayer; they had not yet got any of the liturgical books, so that they could not chant the divine office. Christ's cross was their book and they studied it day and night, at the exhortation and after the example of their father who never stopped talking to them about the cross. When the friars asked him to teach them how to pray, he said, "When you pray, say the Our Father, and We adore you, O Christ, in all your churches in the whole world and we thank you, because by your holy cross you redeemed the world."

ST. BONAVENTURE, *MAJOR LIFE OF ST. FRANCIS*

DAY 30
We Can Rely on God's Provident Care

Better to trust in the Lord
than rely on human help.
Better to trust in the Lord
than rely on generous hearts.

PSALM 118:8-9

MORNING READING

When they had finished begging, [St. Francis and Brother Massea] came together to eat somewhere outside the village. They found nothing but the dry ground to put their begged food on, because that region was quite bare of stones. However, with God's help they came to a spring, and beside it there was a fine broad stone, which made them very happy. And each of them placed on the stone all the pieces of bread he had acquired. And when St. Francis saw that Brother Masseo's pieces of bread were more numerous and better and bigger than his, he was filled with intense joy because of his longing for poverty, and he said: "Oh, Brother Masseo, we do not deserve such a great treasure as this!" And he repeated those words several times, raising his voice each time.

Brother Masseo replied: "Dear Father, how can this be called a treasure when there is such poverty and such a lack of things that are necessary? For here we have no cloth, no knife, no dish, no bowl, no house, no table, no waiter, no waitress."

St. Francis answered: "That is what I consider a great treasure—where nothing has been prepared by human labor. But everything here has been supplied by Divine Providence, as is evident in the begged bread, the fine stone table, and the clear spring. Therefore, I want us to pray to God that he may make us love with all our hearts the very noble treasure of holy poverty, which has God as provider."

THE LITTLE FLOWERS OF SAINT FRANCIS

And in this he showed me something small, no bigger than a hazel-nut, lying in the palm of my hand, and I perceived that it was as round as any ball. I looked at it and thought: What can this be? And I was given this general answer: It is everything which is made. I was amazed that it could last, for I thought that it was so little that it could suddenly fall into nothing. And I was answered in my under-standing: It lasts and always will, because God loves it; and thus everything has being through the love of God.

In this little thing I saw three properties. The first is that God made it, the second is that he loves it, the third is that God preserves it.

JULIAN OF NORWICH

FOR REFLECTION

Lord Jesus, help me trust your loving care in my own life in times of need as well as times of plenty.

[Editor's note: Some of the Friars Ministers thought St. Francis' insis-tence on absolute poverty was unreasonable. They asked him to recon-sider, and at least allow the order to own some things in common. Francis took their request to Jesus in prayer. His response left no doubt about his understanding of God's will in the matter.]

EVENING READING

And Christ at once answered him, saying, "It is my will to with-hold all things from them, both in general and in particular. I will always be ready to provide for this family, however great it may become, and I will always cherish it so long as it shall trust in me."

MIRROR OF PERFECTION

We Are Changed by Sharing Jesus' Cross

Creator, reshape my heart,
God, steady my spirit.
Do not cast me aside
stripped of your holy spirit.

PSALM 51:12-13

MORNING READING

Led by the Spirit, he went in and fell down before the crucifix in devout and humble supplication; and smitten by unusual visitations, he found himself other than he had been when he entered. While he was thus affected, something unheard-of before happened to him: the painted image of Christ crucified moved its lips and spoke. Calling him by name it said: "Francis, go, repair my house, which, as you see, is falling completely to ruin." Trembling, Francis was not a little amazed and became almost deranged by these words. He prepared himself to obey and gave himself completely to the fulfillment of this command. But since he felt that the change he had undergone was beyond expression, it is becoming that we should be silent about what he could not express. From then on compassion for the crucified was rooted in his holy soul, and, as it can be piously supposed, the stigmata of the venerable passion were deeply imprinted in his heart, though not as yet upon his flesh.

THOMAS OF CELANO, *THE SECOND LIFE OF ST. FRANCIS*

I have been crucified with Christ; it is no longer I who live, but Christ who lives in me; and the life I now live in the flesh I live by faith in the Son of God, who loved me and gave himself for me.

GALATIANS 2:20

FOR REFLECTION

Lord Jesus, I am tempted to keep your suffering and horrible death at arms' length. Come into the depths of my spirit and transform me with your boundless love.

EVENING READING

One morning two years before his death, about the feast of the Exaltation of the Cross, while he was praying on the side of a mountain named La Verna, there appeared to him a seraph in the beautiful figure of a crucified man, having his hands and feet extended as though on a cross, and clearly showing the face of Jesus Christ. Two wings met above his head, two covered the rest of his body to the feet, and two were spread as in flight.

When the vision passed, the soul of Francis was afire with love; and on his body there appeared the wonderful impression of the wounds of our Lord Jesus Christ. Blessed Francis did all in his power to hide these wounds, not wishing that God's gift should be seen by men; but he could not hide this gift entirely, and it became known to his intimate companions.

LEGEND OF THE THREE COMPANIONS

In Our Darkest Days, We Turn to the Lord

Grief consumes my life,
sighs fill my days...
Forgotten like the dead,
I am a shattered jar.
But I trust in you, Lord.
I say, "You are my God,
my life is in your hands."

PSALM 31:11, 13, 15-16

MORNING READING

Two years before his death, while he was staying at S. Damian in a cell made of rush-mats, he was suffering intensely from his disease of the eyes, and for more than fifty days he could not bear the light of day, or even firelight. And in order to increase both his affliction and his merit, God allowed a horde of mice to infest the walls of his cell, and they ran over and around him day and night, so that he could neither pray nor rest. Even when he was eating, they climbed onto his table and worried him greatly, so that both he and his companions clearly recognized it as a temptation by the devil.

So one night, tormented by so many troubles and feeling sorry for himself, he prayed inwardly, "Lord, look on me and help me in my troubles, and give me strength to bear them patiently."

MIRROR OF PERFECTION

Why restless, why cast down, my soul?
  Hope still; and thou shalt sing
The praise of him who is thy God,
  Thy health's eternal spring.

PSALM XI
THE BOOK OF HYMNS

FOR REFLECTION

O, Comforter, you know my heart. You know my struggle. Give me faith to trust in your saving help when I can do nothing.

[Editor's note: St. Francis was deeply troubled by some of the brothers' departure from the strict observance of his Rule.]

EVENING READING

For he saw many pursuing offices of authority, and despising their rashness, he sought to recall them from this pestilence by his example. He used to say that it was a good and acceptable thing before God to exercise the care of others and that it was becoming that they should undertake the care of souls who would seek in it nothing of themselves but who would attend always to the divine will in all things. Those, namely, who would put nothing ahead of their own salvation and who would pay no heed to the applause of their subjects but only to their advancement; who would seek not display before men, but glory before God. He was filled with sorrow that some had left their *former works* and had forgotten their earlier simplicity after they had found new things. Wherefore he grieved over those who were once intent upon higher things with their whole desire but who had descended to base and vile things, and had left the true joys to rōam and wander amid frivolous and inane things in the field of empty freedom. He prayed therefore that God's mercy might free these sons and asked most earnestly that they might be kept in the grace *that had been given to them.*

THOMAS OF CELANO, *THE FIRST LIFE OF ST. FRANCIS*

We Share in Jesus' Suffering

I bear shame and insult
because I bear your name.
Insults meant for you
now fall on me.

PSALM 69:8, 10

MORNING READING

He prayed unceasingly with tears and fasting, not relying on his own industry or virtue, but placing all his trust in God; and although he was still in the darkness of the world the Lord filled his soul with ineffable joy and a wonderful light. Glowing with this inner radiance he left the cave, ready to face the insults and blows of his persecutors, and lightheartedly he took the road to Assisi. Trusting in Christ, his heart divinely aflame, Francis now reproached himself for his sloth and vain fears.

When his friends and relatives saw him, they covered him with insults, calling him a fool and a madman, and hurling stones and mud at him. Seeing him so changed, they thought he must be out of his mind.

But God's servant paid no heed to all this; unmoved by insults, he thanked almighty God for everything.

LEGEND OF THE THREE COMPANIONS

When the honeymoon is over—when sickness and difficulties come to our family, when we lose our jobs, fail to acquire that which we greatly desire, suffer the loss of someone we dearly love—when these and other sufferings come to us, we should remember our cousins in creation, the grapevines. We must learn to trust that we will be pruned at the "proper" time by the Divine Vineyard Keeper and that the primary purpose of this suffering is creative. Each pain in life is but a preparation for the final and ultimate pruning when we will be radically cut back—all the way to the ground in our own death. We can embrace that last great adventure without fear if we have, without fear, allowed the divine pruning knife to touch our lives and our loves. From this last and most creative pruning of all, we will come forth in the full-bodied perfection of our resurrection.

EDWARD HAYS

FOR REFLECTION

Lord Jesus, "Suffering Servant," give me courage to willingly accept the suffering that comes because I follow you.

EVENING READING

If you were the most handsome and the richest man in the world, and could work wonders and drive out devils, all that would be something extrinsic to you; it would not belong to you and you could not boast of it. But there is one thing of which we can all boast; we can boast of our humiliations (cf. 2 Cor 12:15) and in taking up daily the holy cross of our Lord Jesus Christ.

Look at the Good Shepherd, my brothers. To save his sheep he endured the agony of the cross. They followed him in trials and persecutions, in ignominy, hunger, and thirst, in humiliations and temptations, and so on. And for this God rewarded them with eternal life.

THE ADMONITIONS

DAY 34
Victory Over Ourselves
Is a Moment of Grace

I consider my ways
and return to yours.
I am more than eager
to do what you command.

PSALM 119:59-60

MORNING READING

This man, endowed with power from on high, was warmed inwardly by a divine fire much more than outwardly by bodily clothing. He cursed those in the order who were clothed with three garments or who, without necessity, used soft garments. Such a necessity, however, that was created by pleasure rather than by reason he would say was a sign of an extinguished spirit. "When the spirit becomes tepid," he said, "and gradually grows cold toward grace, flesh and blood necessarily *seek their own interests.* For what remains," he said, "if the soul does not find its delight, but that the flesh should turn to its delights? And then the animal appetite satisfies the craving of necessity, then carnal feeling forms the conscience." And he would add: "Suppose a real necessity comes upon my brother, or some want takes hold of him; if he is quick to satisfy it and thereby to put it a long way away from him, what reward will he receive? He had indeed an opportunity of gaining merit, but he deliberately proved that it did not please him."

THOMAS OF CELANO, *THE SECOND LIFE OF ST. FRANCIS*

Francis Bernardone saw his fear coming up the road towards him; the fear that comes from within and not without; though it stood white and horrible in the sunlight. For once in the long rush of his life his soul must have stood still. Then he sprang from his horse, knowing nothing between stillness and swiftness, and rushed on the leper and threw his arms round him.

G.K. CHESTERTON

FOR REFLECTION

God, the source of all life, give me faith and courage to confront the things I most dread. Breaking the grip of fear frees me to be immersed more completely in your love.

EVENING READING

So, one day, with great fervor he took a bowl and went through the streets of the city begging for alms from door to door just as he had described the begging of the poor. People dropped a variety of scraps into the bowl; and knowing what his former life had been, many were exceedingly astonished at such self-degradation and at seeing him so completely changed.

When it came to eating the contents of the bowl, Francis' stomach turned, for he had never seen such a mess, let alone tried to eat it. At last, making a great effort, he started to gulp it down, and it seemed to him the most delicious food in the world. His heart leaped with joy and he thanked God, for he realized that, thought weak and afflicted in body, he was able to endure anything, however hard, for the love of the Lord. He praised and thanked God who had changed what was bitter into sweetness and had comforted him in so many ways. He also asked the priest, from then onwards, not to procure or prepare any more food for him.

LEGEND OF THE THREE COMPANIONS

God's Healing Spirit Can Shine Through Us

The troubled call out; God hears,
saves them from all distress.
God stays near broken hearts,
heals the wounded spirit.

PSALM 34:18-19

MORNING READING

Blessed Francis also warned his brothers never to judge or criticize those who live in luxury, eat fastidiously, and indulge in superfluous and splendid clothes; God, he said, is their Lord and ours; he has the power to call them to himself and to justify them. He insisted that the friars should reverence such men as their brothers and masters, and they are indeed brothers since they are children of the same Creator; while they are our masters since they help the good to do penance by giving them what is necessary to the body. To this blessed Francis added: "The general behavior of the friars among people must be such that all who see or hear them may be drawn to glorify our heavenly Father and to praise him devoutly." His great desire was that he and his brothers should abound in the good works for which men give glory and praise to God.

He also said to the brothers: "Since you speak of peace, all the more so must you have it in your hearts. Let none be provoked to anger or scandal by you, but rather may they be drawn to peace and good will, to benignity and concord through your gentleness. We have been called to heal wounds, to unite what has fallen apart, and to bring home those who have lost their way. Many who may seem to us to be children of the Devil will still become Christ's disciples."

LEGEND OF THE THREE COMPANIONS

When a sunbeam falls on a transparent substance, the substance itself becomes brilliant and radiates light from itself. So too Spirit-bearing souls, illumined by him, finally become spiritual themselves, and their grace is sent forth to others.

ST. BASIL THE GREAT OF CAESAREA

FOR REFLECTION

O Mender of Souls, you reach out through us, broken as we may be, to touch and heal your children, to bring peace to a world fallen apart. Open my heart to your restoring presence, not for my good alone, but for those you can reach through me.

[Editor's note: In his youth, Francis eagerly joined the military battle that was fought between Assisi and Perugia. During the war he was captured and held in prison. The following story is told about his conduct while in prison.]

EVENING READING

There was at that time among his fellow prisoners a certain proud and completely unbearable knight whom the rest were determined to shun, but Francis' patience was not disturbed. He put up with the unbearable knight and brought the others to peace with him. Capable of every grace, a chosen vessel of virtues, he poured out his gifts on all sides.

THOMAS OF CELANO, *THE SECOND LIFE OF ST. FRANCIS*

Called to Be Servants

We Serve Others for the Love of God

The Lord bends down
to see heaven and earth,
to raise the weak from the dust
and lift the poor from the mire,
to seat them with princes
in the company of their leaders.

PSALM 113:6-8

MORNING READING

His tender love made him the brother of all creatures, and so it is
no wonder that the love of Christ should unite him even more
closely with those who bear the image of the Maker and are
redeemed by the blood of their Creator. He would not think himself Christ's lover, if he did not compassionate the souls whom he
redeemed. He used to say that nothing should take precedence
over the salvation of souls, because it was for souls that the only-
begotten Son of God hung upon the Cross. It was for souls that he
wrestled in prayer, for souls that he was so active in preaching, and
it was for them that he went beyond all limits in giving good example. When he was reproached for his excessive austerity, he
would reply that he was intended to be an example for others; his
innocent body, which had voluntarily become subject to the spirit,
needed no punishment for sin, yet for the sake of good example, he
inflicted frequent penances on it. It was solely for the sake of others
that "he kept to the paths that are hard to follow" (Ps 16:4). He
used to say, "I may speak with every tongue that men and angels
use; yet, if I lack charity (1 Cor 13:1-3) and fail to set others an
example of virtue, I am of little use to them and none to myself."

ST. BONAVENTURE, *MAJOR LIFE OF ST. FRANCIS*

A young village girl told me, when I am about to talk to anyone, I picture to myself Jesus Christ and how gracious and friendly he was to everyone.

JOHN VIANNEY

FOR REFLECTION

Jesus, source of all compassion, help me see your face in the faces of those around me. As you have loved me extravagantly, give me the grace to share that love freely with those in need.

EVENING READING

Although a merchant, he squandered his wealth, never counting the cost. Once day when he was in the shop selling cloth, a beggar came in and asked for alms for the love of God; but Francis was so intent on the business of making money that he gave nothing to the poor man. Then, enlightened by divine grace, he accused himself harshly, saying: "If that beggar had made his request in the name of some great prince, you would surely have given him what he asked; how much more so you should have done it when he begged in the name of the King of kings and Lord of all!" Taught by this experience, he resolved in his heart never again to refuse anything that might be asked of him in the name of God.

LEGEND OF THE THREE COMPANIONS

DAY 37
We Must Be an Example to Others

Let your loveliness shine on us,
and bless the work we do,
bless the work of our hands.

PSALM 90:17

MORNING READING

In those days, Blessed Francis was living at the hermitage of St. Eleutherius, not far from Contigliano, in the district of Rieti. Since he was wearing but one tunic and it was extremely cold, he was obliged to line the inside of it; so did his companion. His body felt some relief from this. A short time after, as he had just finished his prayer, overjoyed, he said to his companion: "I must be a model and an example to all the brothers. Therefore, although my body needs a lined tunic, I must think of my brothers who are experiencing the same need and who do not have or cannot procure for themselves a like tunic. I must therefore put myself in their place and share their privations, so that they may endure them patiently because they see the way I live."

LEGEND OF PERUGIA

(Our Lord speaks:) "One of the reasons why I wanted to be poorer than the poorest worker was because I came to teach men to despise honors, to despise this world's goods, and because I wanted to give them an example of the most extreme poverty and the most profound abasement. Do the same thing. Your reasons will be the same as mine, with one last one: it is part of your vocation to proclaim the Gospel from the rooftops, not by what you say, but by how you live."

BROTHER CHARLES DE FOUCAULD

FOR REFLECTION

Most Holy God, out of love for us, you chose to leave the splendor of eternity and enter into our world, with its limits of time and space. Your very coming is the ultimate expression of selfless love. You taught not only by words, but also by example. Bless my efforts to follow your example, and to give witness to the Truth in how I live my own life.

EVENING READING

Saint Francis being already full of the grace of the Holy Spirit called the six brothers together in the wood surrounding Saint Mary of the Angels where they often gathered to pray; and there he foretold many future things. "Dear Brothers, let us consider our vocation, and how God, in his great mercy, called us not only for our salvation but for that of many; and to this end we are to go through the world exhorting all men and women by our example as well as by our words to do penance for their sins, and to live keeping in mind the commandments of God." And he added: "Do not be afraid to preach penance even though we appear ignorant and of no account. Put your trust in God who overcame the world; hope steadfastly in him who, by the Holy Spirit, speaks through you to exhort all to be converted to him and to observe his commandments."

LEGEND OF THE THREE COMPANIONS

We Are Called to Be Servants

Who are we that you care for us?
Why give a thought to mortals?
We are little more than breath;
our days, fleeting shadows.

PSALM 144:3-4

MORNING READING

Humility is the guardian and the ornament of all virtues. If the spiritual building does not rest upon it, it will fall to ruin, though it seems to be growing. This virtue filled Francis in a more copious abundance, so that nothing should be wanting to a man adorned with so many gifts. In his own opinion, he was nothing but a sinner, despite the fact that he was the ornament and splendor of all sanctity. He tried to build himself up upon this virtue, so that he would lay the foundation he had learned from Christ. Forgetting the things he had gained, he set before his eyes only his failings in the conviction that he lacked more than he had gained.

He was humble in dress, more humble in conviction, most humble in reputation. This prince of God was not known as anyone's superior except by this brightest jewel alone, namely, that among the lesser he was the least.

THOMAS OF CELANO, THE SECOND LIFE OF ST. FRANCIS

Then the mother of the sons of Zebedee came up to him, with her sons, and kneeling before him she asked him for something. And he said to her, "What do you want?" She said to him, "Command that these two sons of mine may sit, one at your right hand and one at your left, in your kingdom." But Jesus answered, "You do not know what you are asking. Are you able to drink the cup that I am to drink?" They said to him, "We are able." He said to them, "You will drink my cup, but to sit at my right hand and at my left is not mine to grant, but it is for those for whom it has been prepared by my Father." And when the ten heard it, they were indignant at the two brothers. But Jesus called them to him and said, "You know that the rulers of the Gentiles lord it over them, and their great men exercise authority over them. It shall not be so among you; but whoever would be great among you must be your servant, and whoever would be first among you must be your slave; even as the Son of man came not to be served but to serve, and to give his life as a ransom for many."

MATTHEW 20:20-28

FOR REFLECTION

I can easily be proud of my accomplishments or positions and forget that whatever I have been given is not mine, but is yours to be used for the service of others. Lord, teach me true humility.

EVENING READING

I did *not come to be served but to serve* (Mt 20:28), our Lord tells us. Those who are put in charge of others should be no prouder of their office than if they had been appointed to wash the feet of their confrères. They should be no more upset at the loss of their authority than they would be if they were deprived of the task of washing feet. The more they are upset, the greater the risk they incur to their souls.

THE ADMONITIONS

Friendship Rests on the Common Love of God

We praise you God,
and give you thanks.
You are present to us
as we tell your wonders.

PSALM 75:2

MORNING READING

When St. Francis was staying in Assisi, he often visited St. Clare and consoled her with holy advice. And as she had a very great desire to eat a meal with him once, she asked him several times to give her that consolation. But St. Francis always refused to grant her that favor.

So it happened that his companions, perceiving St. Clare's desire, said to St. Francis: "Father, it seems to us that this strictness is not according to divine charity—that you do not grant this request of Sister Clare, a virgin so holy and dear to God, in such a little thing as eating with you."

Then St. Francis replied: "Since it seems so to you, I agree. But in order to give her greater pleasure, I want this meal to be at St. Mary of the Angels, for she has been cloistered at San Damiano for a long time and she will enjoy seeing once more for a while the Place of St. Mary where she was shorn and made a spouse of the Lord Jesus Christ. So we will eat there together, in the name of the Lord."

LITTLE FLOWERS OF ST. FRANCIS

A friend is that other person with whom we can share our solitude, our silence, and our prayer. A friend is that other person with whom we can look at a tree and say, "Isn't that beautiful," or sit on the beach and silently watch the sun disappear under the horizon. With a friend we don't have to say or do something special. With a friend we can be still and know that God is there with both of us.

HENRI NOUWEN

FOR REFLECTION

Jesus, Friend, thank you for the companions you have given to me. As we journey through life together, help us remember that the love we share has its roots in your own love for us. When we are together, enjoying each other's company and support, may we also celebrate your presence with us.

EVENING READING

And she came to St. Mary of the Angels. And first she reverently and humbly greeted the Blessed Virgin Mary before her altar, where she had been shorn and received the veil. And then they devoutly showed her around the place until it was mealtime. Meanwhile St. Francis had the table prepared on the bare ground, as was his custom.

And when it was time to eat, St. Francis and St. Clare sat down together, and one of his companions with St. Clare's companion, and all his other companions were grouped around that humble table. But at the first course St. Francis began to speak about God in such a sweet and holy and profound and divine and marvelous way that he himself and St. Clare and her companion and all the others who were at that poor little table were rapt in God by the overabundance of divine grace that descended upon them.

LITTLE FLOWERS OF ST. FRANCIS

DAY 40
We Are to Reflect the
Motherly Love of God

Your maternal love
surrounds me, Lord.
Your sure and tender care
protects me always.

PSALM 40:12

MORNING READING

Not more than three or at most four friars should go together to a
hermitage to lead a religious life there. Two of these should act as
mothers, with the other two, or the other one, as their children.
The mothers are to lead the life of Martha; the other two, the life
of Mary Magdalen.

The friars who are mothers must be careful to stay away from
outsiders and in obedience to their custos keep their sons away
from them, so that no one can speak to them. Now and then, the
sons should exchange places with the mothers, according to whatever arrangement seems best suited for the moment.

RELIGIOUS LIFE IN HERMITAGES

From this it follows that as truly as God is our Father, so truly is God
our Mother.... To the property of motherhood belong nature, love, wis-
dom and knowledge, and this is God.... The kind, loving mother who
knows and sees the need of her child guards it very tenderly, as the
nature and condition of motherhood will have. And always as the
child grows in age and in stature, she acts differently, but she does
not change her love. And when it is even older, she allows it to be chas-
tised to destroy its faults, so as to make the child receive virtues and

grace. This work, with everything which is lovely and good, our Lord performs in those by whom it is done. So he is our Mother in nature by the operation of grace in the lower part, for love of the higher part.

JULIAN OF NORWICH

FOR REFLECTION

God, our Mother, from the time you formed me in my mother's womb you have been mindful of me. You are always present, pouring out grace to nurture and sustain me, to bring me back when I stray. Thank you for your unwavering care. Help me share your maternal love with those who need to feel your warm, accepting embrace.

EVENING READING

During the period when blessed Francis began to have brethren, and was living with them at Rivo Torto near Assisi, one night while all the brethren were asleep one of the friars cried out, saying, "I am dying!"

Startled and frightened, all the friars awoke. Blessed Francis got up and said, "Rise, brothers, and light a lamp." And when it was lit, he said, "Who was it who said, 'I am dying'?"

The friar answered, "It is I." And he said, "What is the matter, brother? How are you dying?" And he said, "I am dying of hunger."

The holy Father at once ordered food to be brought, and having great charity and discretion, he ate with him lest he should be ashamed to eat alone; and, at his wish, all the other friars joined them.

MIRROR OF PERFECTION

DAY 41
We Care for Others As God Cares for Us

God shelters you from evil,
securing your life.
God watches over you near and far,
now and always.

PSALM 121:7-8

MORNING READING

Once it happened that a certain brother uttered a word of invective against a certain poor man who had asked for an alms, saying to him: "See, perhaps you are a rich man pretending to be poor." Hearing this, the father of the poor, St. Francis, was greatly saddened, and he severely rebuked the brother who had said such a thing and commanded him to strip himself before the poor man and, kissing his feet, beg pardon of him. For, he was accustomed to say: "Who curses a poor man does an injury to Christ, whose noble image he wears, the image of him who made himself poor for us in this world." Frequently, therefore, when he found the poor burdened down with wood or other things, he offered his own shoulders to help them, though his shoulders were very weak.

THOMAS CELANO, THE FIRST LIFE OF ST. FRANCIS

If we are able to enter the church day and night and implore God to hear our prayers, how careful should we be to hear and grant the petitions of our neighbor in need.

ST. JOHN THE ALMSGIVER (C.560–C.619)

FOR REFLECTION

Creator of the universe, that you are ever present to me and mindful of my need is a gift I cannot comprehend; yet I believe it is so. The favor of your love and concern is given not only to nurture and heal me, but also to flow through me to others.

[Editor's note: Francis had constant trouble with his eyes. Once, he asked the brothers to invite the doctor who was treating his eyes to join them for dinner. The brothers were hesitant because they had such meager offerings. Francis insisted.]

EVENING READING

The doctor, who was standing by, said: "Dearest brothers, I will consider your poverty a real delicacy." The brothers hurried and placed upon the table all they had in their storeroom, namely, a little bread, not much wine, and, that they might eat a bit more sumptuously, the kitchen provided some vegetables. Meanwhile the table of the Lord had compassion on the table of his servants. There was a knock at the door and it was answered quickly. Behold, a certain woman offered them a basket full of fine bread, fishes and lobster pies, honey and grapes. The table of the poor brothers rejoiced at the sight of these things, and keeping the common things for the next day, they ate the better things that day. With a sigh the doctor spoke, saying: "Brothers, neither you nor we of the world know this man's sanctity as we should." At length they were satisfied, but the miracle gave them greater satisfaction than the banquet. Thus the eye of the Father never despises his children, but rather, the more poor they are, the more richly does providence provide for them. The poor man is provided with a more abundant table than the tyrant, inasmuch as God is more generous in his gifts than man.

THOMAS OF CELANO, *THE SECOND LIFE OF ST. FRANCIS*

We Are Called to Give Generously

Do not worry about wealth,
when someone else becomes rich.
You cannot take it to your grave,
wealth is worth nothing in death.
No matter how wealthy,
no matter how many tell you,
"My, how well you have done,"
the rich all join the dead
never to see light again.

PSALM 49:17-20

MORNING READING

Even as a young man Francis had an open-handed sympathy for the poor which God had inspired in his heart. This bore him company as he grew up and filled his heart with such generosity that he refused to turn a deaf ear to the Gospel and resolved to give alms to everyone who approached him, especially if it was for the love of God. One time he was caught in a rush of business and, contrary to his custom, he sent away a beggar who had begged an alms for love of God without giving him anything. Then he realized what he had done and he ran after him immediately and gave him a generous alms. There and then he promised God that he would never again refuse anyone who asked for love of him, as long as he had anything to give.

ST. BONAVENTURE, *MAJOR LIFE OF ST. FRANCIS*

Wherever men are to be found who are in want of food and drink, of clothing, housing, medicine, work, education, the means necessary for leading a truly human life, wherever there are men racked by misfortune or illness, men suffering exile or imprisonment, Christian charity should go in search of them and find them out, comfort them with devoted care and give them the helps that will relieve their needs. This obligation binds first and foremost the more affluent individuals and nations.

VATICAN COUNCIL II: THE CONCILIAR DOCUMENTS DECREE
ON THE APOSTOLATE OF LAY PEOPLE-776

FOR REFLECTION

Jesus, many in the world are crying for help. Sometimes I am impatient. Yet, you told us not to store up earthly treasure, for our hearts will be where our treasures lie. Help me shift my focus from myself to those in need. My possessions will mean little when I am finished with life on earth. "How well have you loved?" will be the question you ask. Jesus, help me love.

EVENING READING

We must be charitable, too, and humble, and give alms, because they wash the stains of sin from our souls. We lose everything which we leave behind us in this world; we can bring with us only the right to a reward for our charity and the alms we have given. For these we shall receive a reward, a just retribution from God.

LETTER TO ALL THE FAITHFUL

We Are Called to Show God's Mercy

Your mercy, Lord, spans the sky;
your faithfulness soars among the clouds.
Your integrity towers like a mountain;
your justice runs deeper than the sea.
Lord, you embrace all life:
How we prize your tender mercy!

PSALM 36:6-8

[Editor's note: Francis visited a hermitage frequented by known robbers, who sometimes came out of hiding to ask the brothers for alms. Some brothers thought they should refuse the brigands. Others believed that simple hunger was driving these men to their misdeeds and desired to give them alms, advising them to change their ways. Knowing the robbers could not change all at once, Francis gave the friars a plan. First, he told them to humbly serve a meal to the robbers and have them promise never to harm another. Later, the brothers should prepare a more elaborate meal and serve it to the robbers. After that meal, Francis instructed the brothers to address the robbers, saying:]

MORNING READING

"'Why do you stay here all day long dying of hunger, suffering so much, doing so much evil in thought and in act? You will lose your souls if you are not converted to the Lord. It would be much better for you to serve God who will give you what you need for your bodies in this world and who in the end will save your souls.' And the Lord in his goodness will inspire them to be converted because of the humility and charity that you have shown them."

The brothers got up and did all that blessed Francis had coun-

selled them to do. Through the mercy and grace of God, the robbers listened and fulfilled the brothers' requests one by one.
Touched by their charity and affability, they even carried wood on
their backs to the hermitage. By the mercy of God and thanks to
the charity and goodness to which the brothers had given witness,
some entered the Order, while others were converted to penance
and promised while holding the hands of the brothers, never to do
evil in the future but to live by the work of their hands. The
brothers of the hermitage and those who heard the good news
were full of admiration as they considered the holiness of blessed
Francis and the quick conversion of these faithless and lawless
men, as foretold by him.

LEGEND OF PERUGIA

*My brothers, Christ made love the stairway that would enable all
Christians to climb to heaven. Hold fast to it, therefore, in all sin-
cerity, give one another practical proof of it, and by your progress,
make your ascent together.*

ST. FULGENTIUS

FOR REFLECTION

Compassionate One, I am overwhelmed by your eagerness to pardon my sins and gather me into your embrace. Humbled by your
mercy, help me extend that same mercy to those who journey with
me toward eternal life.

EVENING READING

Our Lord says in the Gospel, *Love your enemies* (Mt 5:44). A man
really loves his enemy when he is not offended by the injury done
to himself, but for love of God feels burning sorrow for the sin his
enemy has brought on his own soul, and proves his love in a practical way.

THE ADMONITIONS

Whatever We Do to the Least One, We Do to the Lord

He will rescue the poor at their call,
those no one speaks for.
Those no one cares for
he hears and will save,
save their lives from violence,
lives precious in his eyes.

PSALM 72:12-14

MORNING READING

St. Francis was filled with such a spirit of gentle compassion, which came to him from the Source of Mercy itself, that he seemed to have a mother's tenderness in caring for the sufferings of those in misery. He was kind by nature and the love of Christ merely intensified this. His whole soul went out to the sick and the poor, and where he could not offer material assistance he lavished his affection; the poverty or deprivation he saw in anyone he immediately referred to Christ in his heartfelt compassion. In every poor person he met, he saw the image of Christ and he insisted on giving them anything which had been given to him, even if he had urgent need of it; indeed, he believed that he was bound to give it to them, just as if it belonged to them. He spared nothing—cloaks, habits, books, or altarcloths—as long as he was in a position to do so, he gave them all to the poor. He wanted nothing more than to spend and be spent himself, in order to fulfill the duty of being compassionate towards others.

ST. BONAVENTURE, *MINOR LIFE OF ST. FRANCIS*

When the Son of man comes in his glory, and all the angels with him, then he will sit on his glorious throne. Before him will be gathered all the nations, and he will separate them one from another as a shepherd separates the sheep from the goats, and he will place the sheep at his right hand, but the goats at the left. Then the King will say to those at his right hand, "Come, O blessed of my Father, inherit the kingdom prepared for you from the foundation of the world; for I was hungry and you gave me food, I was thirsty and you gave me drink, I was a stranger and you welcomed me, I was naked and you clothed me, I was sick and you visited me, I was in prison and you came to me." Then the righteous will answer him, "Lord, when did we see thee hungry and feed thee, or thirsty and give thee drink? And when did we see thee a stranger and welcome thee, or naked and clothe thee? And when did we see thee sick or in prison and visit thee?" And the King will answer them, "Truly, I say to you, as you did it to one of the least of these my brethren, you did it to me."

MATTHEW 25:31-40

FOR REFLECTION

Jesus, share with me your compassionate heart. Help me recognize your face in those of my sisters and brothers.

EVENING READING

When you see a poor man, you must consider the one in whose name he comes, namely, Christ, who took upon himself our poverty and weakness. The poverty and sickness of this man are, therefore, a mirror in which we ought to contemplate lovingly the poverty and weakness which our Lord Jesus Christ suffered in his body to save the human race.

LEGEND OF PERUGIA

Creation: A Ladder to God

We Delight in God's Creatures

This is the day the Lord has made,
let us rejoice and be glad.

PSALM 118:24

MORNING READING

Once when Saint Francis was about to eat with Brother Leo he was greatly delighted to hear a nightingale singing. So he suggested to his companion that they should also sing praise to God alternately with the bird. While Leo was pleading that he was no singer, Francis lifted up his voice and, phrase by phrase, sang his duet with the nightingale. Thus they continued from Vespers to Lauds, until the Saint had to admit himself beaten by the bird. Thereupon the nightingale flew on to his hand, where he praised it to the skies and fed it. Then he gave it his blessing and it flew away.

A NEW FIORETTI

All things bright and beautiful
All creatures great and small,
All things wise and wonderful,
The Lord God made them all.

Each little flower that opens,
Each little bird that sings,
He made their glowing colours,
He made their tiny wings.

He gave us eyes to see them,
And lips that we may tell
How great is God Almighty,
Who has made all things well.

FOLLIOTT SANDFORD PIERPOINT
"ALL THINGS BRIGHT AND BEAUTIFUL," VV. 1, 2, 7

FOR REFLECTION

The concerns and activities of life occupy my time, and I forget to take pleasure from the wonder of your creatures. Holy One, open my eyes to the beauty and marvelous variety of all living things.

EVENING READING

When Francis arrived at the hermitage on Mount La Verna to keep the fast in honor of St. Michael the Archangel, a flock of birds of all kinds wheeled about his cell, singing and showing their joy at his arrival. They seemed to be inviting their father to stay with them. When he saw them, Francis remarked to his companion, "I see that it is God's will we should stay here, our sisters the birds are so glad to see us." During his stay there, a falcon which was nesting at that spot became a great friend of his and woke him every night with its song just at the time he used to rise to say the office. The saint was delighted; by its anxious care for him the bird allowed him no time for laziness. But when he needed a longer rest than usual, the falcon had pity on him and did not wake him up so early; as if it had been instructed by God, it would then call him about dawn with its bell-like song.

ST. BONAVENTURE, *MAJOR LIFE OF ST. FRANCIS*

God's Spirit Renews Us
Like Water Renews the Earth

Have mercy, tender God,
forget that I defied you.
Wash away my sin,
cleanse me from my guilt.
You love those centered in truth;
teach me your hidden wisdom.
Wash me with fresh water,
wash me bright as snow.

PSALM 51:3-4, 8-9

MORNING READING

Next to fire he had an especial love for water, because it symbolizes holy penitence and tribulation, and at Baptism the soul is cleansed from its stains and receives its first purification. So whenever he washed his hands he chose a place where the water would not be trodden underfoot as it fell to the ground. For the same reason, whenever he had to walk over rocks, he trod reverently and fearfully, out of love for Christ Who is called *The Rock*: so whenever he recited the psalm *Thou wilt set me high upon a rock*, he used to say with great reverence and devotion, *Thou hast set me up at the foot of the rock.*

MIRROR OF PERFECTION

And why did he call the grace of the Spirit water? Because by water all things subsist; because water brings forth grass and living things; because the water of the showers comes down from heaven; because it comes down one in form, but works in many forms. For one fountain watereth the whole of Paradise, and one and the same rain comes down upon all the world, yet it becomes white in the lily, and red in the rose, and purple in violets and hyacinths, and different and varied in each several kind.... Thus also the Holy Ghost, being one, and of one nature, and indivisible, divides to each his grace, according as he will: and as the dry tree, after partaking of water, puts forth shoots, so also the soul in sin, when it has been through repentance made worthy of the Holy Ghost, brings forth clusters of righteousness.

ST. CYRIL OF JERUSALEM

FOR REFLECTION

Holy Spirit, soak into me like water into parched ground. I am in need of your life-giving sweetness. Cleansing Spirit, fall upon me like rain onto a dusty city. I am in need of your purifying ablution.

EVENING READING

All praise be yours, my Lord, through Brothers Wind and Air,
   And fair and stormy, all the weather's moods,
   By which you cherish all that you have made.
All praise be yours, my Lord, through Sister Water,
   So useful, lowly, precious and pure.

THE CANTICLE OF BROTHER SUN

All Creation Is Illuminated by the Glory of God

Lord our God,
the whole world tells
the greatness of your name.
Your glory reaches
beyond the stars.

I see your handiwork
in the heavens:
the moon and the stars
you set in place.

PSALM 8:2, 4

MORNING READING

Francis sought occasion to love God in everything. He delighted in all the works of God's hands and from the vision of joy on earth his mind soared aloft to the life-giving source and cause of all. In everything beautiful, he saw him who is beauty itself, and he followed his Beloved everywhere by his likeness imprinted on creation; of all creation he made a ladder by which he might mount up and embrace him who is all-desirable. By the power of his extraordinary faith he tasted the Goodness which is the source of all in each and every created thing, as in so many rivulets. He seemed to perceive a divine harmony in the interplay of powers and faculties given by God to his creatures and like the prophet David he exhorted them all to praise God.

ST. BONAVENTURE, *MAJOR LIFE OF ST. FRANCIS*

The transition from the good man to the saint is a sort of revolution; by which one for whom all things illustrate and illuminate God becomes one for whom God illustrates and illuminates all things. It is rather like the reversal whereby a lover might say at first sight that a lady looked like a flower, and say afterwards that all flowers reminded him of his lady. A saint and a poet standing by the same flower might seem to say the same thing; but indeed though they would both be telling the truth, they would be telling different truths. For one the joy of life is a cause of faith, for the other rather a result of faith.

G.K. CHESTERTON

FOR REFLECTION

Without you, nothing exists! Lord, help me see that it is your Being that gives beauty and definition to everything that is.

EVENING READING

We must refer every good to the most high supreme God, acknowledging that all good belongs to him; and we must thank him for it all, because all good comes from him. May the most supreme and high and only true God receive and have and be paid all honor and reverence, all praise and blessing, all thanks and all glory, for to him belongs all good and *no one is good but only God* (Lk 18:19).

THE RULE OF 1221

All Things Turn Our Hearts to God

God speaks: the heavens are made;
God breathes: the stars shine.
God bottles the waters of the sea
and stores them in the deep.
All earth, be astounded,
stand in awe of God.
God speaks: the world is;
God commands: all things appear.

PSALM 33:6-9

MORNING READING

He told the friar who cut and chopped wood for the fire that he must never cut down the whole tree, but remove branches in such a way that part of the tree remained intact, out of love for Christ, who willed to accomplish our salvation on the wood of the cross.

We who were with him have seen him take inward and outward delight in almost every creature, and when he handled or looked at them his spirit seemed to be in heaven rather than on earth. And not long before his death, in gratitude for the many consolations that he had received through creatures, he composed *The Praises of the Lord in His Creatures*, in order to stir the hearts of those who heard them to the praise of God, and to move men to praise the Lord himself in his creatures.

MIRROR OF PERFECTION

Every creature in the world will raise our hearts to God if we look upon it with a good eye.

SAINT FELIX OF CANTALICE

The mind can, through the senses, see the Creator in the creation, as the sun is seen reflected in the waters.

St. Nicodemus of the Holy Mountain

FOR REFLECTION

The wonders of the universe continue to unfold before us. Maker of all that is, your creation fills me with awe. From subatomic particles to distant stars, it hints at your magnificence. No matter what my mind can discover, I will never be able to grasp the mystery and glory that is your being.

EVENING READING

His attitude towards creation was simple and direct, as simple as the gaze of a dove; as he considered the universe, in his pure, spiritual vision, he referred every created thing to the Creator of all. He saw God in everything, and loved and praised him in all creation. By God's generosity and goodness, he possessed God in everything and everything in God. The realization that everything comes from the same source made him call all created things—no matter how insignificant—his brothers and sisters, because they had the same origins as he.

St. Bonaventure, *Minor Life of St. Francis*

We Praise God in Creation

I ponder your splendor and glory
and all your wonderful works.

PSALM 145:5

MORNING READING

For who could ever give expression to the very great affection he bore for all things that are God's? Who would be able to narrate the sweetness he enjoyed while contemplating in creatures the wisdom of their Creator, his power and his goodness? Indeed, he was very often filled with a wonderful and ineffable joy from this consideration while he looked upon the sun, while he beheld the moon, and while he gazed upon the stars and the firmament. O simple piety and pious simplicity! Toward little worms even he glowed with a very great love, for he had read this saying about the Savior: *I am a worm, not a man.* Therefore he picked them up from the road and placed them in a safe place, lest they be crushed by the feet of the passersby. What shall I say of the lower creatures, when he would see to it that the bees would be provided with honey in the winter, or the best wine, lest they should die from the cold? He used to praise in public the perfection of their works and the excellence of their skill, for the glory of God, with such encomiums that he would often spend a whole day in praising them and the rest of creatures. For as of old the three youths in the fiery furnace invited all the elements to praise and glorify the Creator of the universe, so also this man, filled with the spirit of God, never ceased to glorify, praise, and bless the Creator and Ruler of all things in all the elements and creatures.

THOMAS OF CELANO, *THE FIRST LIFE OF ST. FRANCIS*

There is no plant in the ground
But is full of his virtue...
There is no life in the sea,
There is no creature in the river,
There is naught in the firmament,
But proclaims his goodness...
There is no bird on the wing,
There is no star in the sky,
There is nothing beneath the sun,
But proclaims his goodness.
   Jesu! Jesu! Jesu!
   Jesu! meet it were to praise Him.

JESU WHO OUGHT TO BE PRAISED
THE CELTIC VISION

FOR REFLECTION

Maker of all that is, I join my voice to those of your people around this earth in praise for the splendor of your creation.

EVENING READING

Every creature in heaven and on earth and in the depths of the sea should give God praise and glory and honor and blessing (cf. Rv 5:13); he has borne so much for us and has done and will do so much good to us; he is our power and our strength, and he alone is good (cf. Lk 18:19), he alone most high, he alone all-powerful, wonderful, and glorious; he alone is holy and worthy of all praise and blessing for endless ages and ages. Amen.

LETTER TO ALL THE FAITHFUL

DAY 50
God's Creation Remains Faithful

Shout to the Lord, you earth
break into song, into praise!
Let the sea roar with its creatures,
the world and all that live there!
Let rivers clap their hands,
the hills ring out their joy!

PSALM 98:4, 7-8

MORNING READING

How great a gladness do you think the beauty of the flowers brought to his mind when he saw the shape of their beauty and perceived the odor of their sweetness? He used to turn the eye of consideration immediately to the beauty of that flower that comes *from the root of Jesse* and gives light *in the days of spring* and by its fragrance has raised innumerable thousands from the dead. When he found an abundance of flowers, he preached to them and invited them to praise the Lord as though they were endowed with reason. In the same way he exhorted with the sincerest purity cornfields and vineyards, stones and forests and all the beautiful things of the fields, fountains of water and the green things of the gardens, earth and fire, air and wind, to love God and serve him willingly. Finally, he called all creatures *brother*, and in a most extraordinary manner, a manner never experienced by others, he discerned the hidden things of nature with his sensitive heart, as one who had already escaped *into the freedom of the glory of the sons of God.*

THOMAS OF CELANO, *THE FIRST LIFE OF ST. FRANCIS*

It is that faithfulness of the natural world to the Creator that fills those who see with reverence and awe. By its pure reflection of God's artistry and creative power, it moves us to prayer and reveals some facet of the maker to his people. When we open our eyes, ears, and hearts to the wordless chant of praise that arises every day from every created thing, we can join in their prayer. Recognizing their holiness, our own hearts are stirred with the desire to grow in willingness to be, like them, exactly as God has made us to be. Then our "Amen" will rise with theirs, not from our lips alone, but from our being.

MARY VAN BALEN HOLT

FOR REFLECTION

Holy One, only to human beings have you given the possibility of clouding our souls with falseness. Give me the wisdom to discover who you have made me to be, and the willingness to accept that self, with its limitations as well as its possibilities. Then I, too, will praise you not with words but with my existence.

EVENING READING

Above all birds he loved the little lark, known in the language of the country as *lodola capellata* (the hooded lark). He used to say of it, "Sister lark has a hood like a Religious and is a humble bird, for she walks contentedly along the road to find grain, and even if she finds it among rubbish, she pecks it out and eats it. As she flies she praises God very sweetly, like good Religious who despise earthly things, whose *minds are set on the things of heaven*, and whose constant purpose is to praise God."

MIRROR OF PERFECTION

Ordinary Things Can Lead Us to God

Bow down to worship at God's feet,
lift your voice in praise,
"Holy is the Lord!"

PSALM 99:5

MORNING READING

One Lent he had made a little vase, using just the little time he had to spare, so that he would not be completely taken up with it. One day, while he was devoutly saying Tierce, his eyes turned to look at the vessel, and he felt that the interior man was thereby impeded in its fervor. Sorrowful therefore that the voice of his heart had been interrupted in its speaking to the ears of God, when Tierce was finished he said before the listening brothers: "Alas, what a worthless work that has such power over me that it can twist my mind to itself! I will sacrifice it to the Lord, whose sacrifice it has impeded." When he said these words, he took the little vase and threw it into the fire to be burned.

THOMAS OF CELANO, *THE SECOND LIFE OF ST. FRANCIS*

What do I mean by icon?... I am not thinking of the classic definition of the icons so familiar in the Orthodox Church.... My personal definition is much wider, and the simplest way I can put it into words is to affirm that an icon, for me, is an open window to God. An icon is something I can look through and get a wider glimpse of God and God's demands on us, el's mortal children, than I would otherwise.... An icon does not have to be an idol. An icon should give us glimpses of our God, who is both immanent and transcendent, knowable and unknowable. If an icon becomes more important to us than what it reveals of God, then it becomes a golden calf, but this does not need to happen.

MADELEINE L'ENGLE

FOR REFLECTION

Francis found the little vase a distraction only when it drew his attention to itself instead of the beauty or simplicity that could lead his thoughts to the Maker.

Holy One, our world is filled with material objects: tools for our work, necessities, art. Bless us with vision to see into your glory through the ordinary things that fill our lives.

EVENING READING

In that place there was a certain man by the name of John. Blessed Francis sent for this man, and he said to him: "If you want us to celebrate the present feast of our Lord at Greccio, go with haste and diligently prepare what I tell you. For I wish to do something that will recall to memory the little Child who was born in Bethlehem and set before our bodily eyes in some way the inconveniences of his infant needs, how he lay in a manger, how, with an ox and an ass standing by, he lay upon the hay."

The manger was prepared, the hay had been brought, the ox and ass were led in. There simplicity was honored, poverty was exalted, humility was commended, and Greccio was made, as it were, a new Bethlehem.

The people came and were filled with new joy over the new mystery.

THOMAS OF CELANO, THE FIRST LIFE OF ST. FRANCIS

DAY 52
We Appreciate God's Gift of Creation

My soul, bless the Lord,
bless God's holy name!
My soul, bless the Lord,
hold dear all God's gifts.

PSALM 103:1-2

MORNING READING

In the same way he told the friar who cared for the gardens not to cultivate all the ground for vegetables, but to set aside a plot to grow flowers to bloom in their season, out of love for him who is called *The Rose on the plain and the Lily on the mountain slopes.* Indeed, he told the brother-gardener that he should always make a pleasant flower-garden, and cultivate every variety of fragrant herb and flowering plant, so that all who saw the herbs and flowers would be moved to praise God. For every creature proclaims, "God made me for your sake, O man."

MIRROR OF PERFECTION

A tree gives glory to God by being a tree. For in being what God means it to be it is obeying him. It "consents," so to speak, to his creative love.

Therefore each particular being, in its individuality, its concrete nature and entity, with all its own characteristics and its private qualities and its own inviolable identity, gives glory to God by being precisely what he wants it to be here and now, in the circumstances ordained for it by his Love and his infinite Art.

Their inscape is their sanctity. It is the imprint of his wisdom and his reality in them.

The special clumsy beauty of this particular colt on this April day in this field under these clouds is a holiness consecrated to God by his own creative wisdom and it declares the glory of God.

The pale flowers of the dogwood outside this window are saints. The little yellow flowers that nobody notices on the edge of the road are saints looking up into the face of God.

This leaf has its own texture and its own pattern of veins and its own holy shape, and the bass and trout hiding in the deep pools of the river are canonized by their beauty and their strength.

The lakes hidden among the hills are saints, and the sea too is a saint who praises God without interruption in her majestic dance.

THOMAS MERTON

FOR REFLECTION

Maker of all things, freshen my gaze that I might appreciate the magnificence of your creation.

EVENING READING

"These creatures minister to our needs every day; without them we could not live; and through them the human race greatly offends the Creator. Every day we fail to appreciate so great a blessing by not praising as we should the Creator and dispenser of all these gifts."

LEGEND OF PERUGIA

Filled With Praise and Joy

What Is Foolishness to the World
Is Our Glory

To live with you is joy,
to praise you and never stop.

PSALM 84:5

MORNING READING

One day at St. Mary, St Francis called Brother Leo and said: "Brother Leo, write this down."

He answered: "I'm ready."

"Write down what true joy is," he said. "A messenger comes and says that all the masters of theology in Paris have joined the Order—write: that is not true joy. Or all the prelates beyond the mountains—archbishops and bishops, or the King of France and the King of England—write: that is not true joy. Or that my friars have gone to the unbelievers and have converted all of them to the faith; or that I have so much grace from God that I heal the sick and I perform many miracles. I tell you that true joy is not in all those things."

"But what is true joy?"

"I am returning from Perugia and I am coming here at night, in the dark. It is winter time and wet and muddy and so cold that icicles form at the edges of my habit and keep striking my legs, and blood flows from such wounds. And I come to the gate, all covered with mud and cold and ice, and after I have knocked and called for a long time, a friar comes and asks: 'Who are you?' I answer: 'Brother Francis.' And he says: 'Go away. This is not a decent time to be going about. You can't come in.'

"And when I insist again, he replies: 'Go away. You are a simple and uneducated fellow. From now on don't stay with us anymore.

We are so many and so important that we don't need you.'

"But I still stand at the gate and say: 'For the love of God, let me come in tonight.' and he answers: 'I won't. Go to the Crosiers' Place and ask there.'

"I tell you that if I kept patience and was not upset—that is true joy and true virtue and the salvation of the soul."

LITTLE FLOWERS OF ST. FRANCIS
OMNIBUS PUBLISHED IN 1927 BY FATHER BUGHETTI
FROM AN EARLY FOURTEENTH-CENTURY LATIN MANUSCRIPT

When I survey the wondrous Cross,
Where the young Prince of Glory died,
My richest gain I count but loss,
And pour contempt on all my pride.

ISAAC WATTS
"WHEN I SURVEY THE WONDROUS CROSS"

FOR REFLECTION

Jesus, help me seek joy in embracing the foolishness of the cross.

EVENING READING

Two young men once came to the Blessed Francis desiring to be received into the Order. But the Saint, anxious to test their obedience and to find out whether they were really willing to surrender their own wills, took them into the garden and said to them: "Come, and let us plant some cabbages; and as you see me doing, so you must do also." So the Blessed Francis began to plant, putting the cabbages with the roots up in the air and the leaves down under the ground.

Then one of the two men did as Francis was doing, but the other said: "That isn't the way to plant cabbages, father; you're putting them in upside down!" Blessed Francis said to him: "Brother, I see that you are a very learned man; but go your way; you won't do for my Order." So he accepted the one and refused the other.

A NEW FIORETTI

We Praise God for Being God

Before the mountains existed,
before the earth was born,
from age to age you are God.

PSALM 90:2

MORNING READING

Almighty, most high and supreme God, Father, holy and just, Lord, King of heaven and earth, we give you thanks for yourself. Of your own holy will you created all things spiritual and physical, made us in your own image and likeness, and gave us a place in paradise, through your only Son, in the Holy Spirit....

With all our hearts and all our souls, all our minds and all our strength, all our power and all our understanding, with every faculty (cf. Dt 6:5) and every effort, with every affection and all our emotions, with every wish and desire, we should love our Lord and God who has given and gives us everything, body and soul, and all our life. He alone is true God, who is perfect good, all good, every good, the true and supreme good, and he alone is good, loving and gentle, kind and understanding; he alone is holy, just, true, and right; he alone is kind, innocent, pure, and from him, through him, and in him is all pardon, all grace, and all glory for the penitent, the just and the blessed who rejoice in heaven.

THE RULE OF 1221

Editor's Note: Dorothy Day remembers her first memories of God:
It was a Sunday afternoon in the attic. I remember the day was
very chilly, though there were roses and violets and calla lilies
blooming in the garden. My sister and I had been making dolls of
the calla lilies, putting rosebuds for heads at the top of the long

graceful blossom. Then we made perfume, crushing flowers into a bottle with a little water in it. Even now I can remember the peculiar, delicious, pungent smell.

And then I remember we were in the attic. I was sitting behind a table, pretending I was the teacher, reading aloud from a Bible that I had found. Slowly, as I read, a new personality impressed itself on me. I was being introduced to someone and I knew almost immediately that I was discovering God.

I know that I had just really discovered him because it excited me tremendously. It was as though life were fuller, richer, more exciting in every way. Here was someone that I had never really known about before and yet felt to be One who I would never forget, that I would never get away from. The game might grow stale, it might assume new meanings, new aspects, but life would never again be the same. I had made a great discovery.

DOROTHY DAY

FOR REFLECTION

Unknowable One, I stand silent before you and offer you myself. With everything you have made me, I give thanks for the Wonderful Mystery of yourself.

EVENING READING

Most High, Almighty, good Lord,
Thine be the praise, the glory, the honour,
        And all blessing.
To thee alone, Most High, are they due,
        And no man is worthy
        To speak thy name.

FROM *THE SONG OF BROTHER SUN*
IN MIRROR OF PERFECTION

Spiritual Joy Should Fill Our Hearts

If you would be happy:
never walk with the wicked,
never stand with sinners,
never sit among cynics,
but delight in the Lord's teaching
and study it night and day.

PSALM 1:1-2

MORNING READING

St. Francis maintained that the safest remedy against the thousand snares and wiles of the enemy is spiritual joy. For he would say: "Then the devil rejoices most when he can snatch away spiritual joy from a servant of God. He carries dust so that he can throw it into even the tiniest chinks of conscience and soil the candor of mind and purity of life. But when spiritual joy fills hearts," he said, "the serpent throws off his deadly poison in vain. The devils cannot harm the servant of Christ when they see he is filled with holy joy. When, however, the soul is wretched, desolate, and filled with sorrow, it is easily overwhelmed by its sorrow or else it turns to vain enjoyments."

THOMAS OF CELANO, THE SECOND LIFE OF ST. FRANCIS

Saint Francis seems to have been a man who truly found happiness, or perhaps whom happiness found. While every saint is a man or woman of heroic determination, Saint Francis had unusual confidence in the strength of the individual to create a life rich with meaning. He taught his followers not only how to love but how to sing and laugh like a jester, infusing the religious experience with new-found joy. He told them that "spiritual joy is as necessary to the soul as blood to the body." He radiated this teaching, bringing bliss to all who came into contact with him.

What was the secret to Saint Francis' sense of fulfillment? He strived to live each moment as a gift, as a blessing.

ANNE GORDON

FOR REFLECTION

Source of Happiness, open my heart to the gifts you bestow every day. Direct the eyes of my spirit to look out toward others and the good in the world you created, that I may be filled with your holy joy.

EVENING READING

These four brothers were united in immense spiritual joy and gladness; but in order to advance their work, they separated. Blessed Francis, taking with him Brother Giles, went into the Marches of Ancona, while the others took another direction. As they were journeying through the Marches, they rejoiced greatly in the Lord, and Francis in a loud, clear voice sang the praise of God in French, glorifying and blessing the goodness of the Almighty. Their hearts indeed overflowed with joy, as though they had found the greatest treasure in the evangelical field of holy poverty; and for her sake they gladly and freely considered all temporal things as dung.

LEGEND OF THE THREE COMPANIONS

A Holy Zeal Leads Us to God

Come, sing with joy to God,
shout to our savior, our rock.
Enter God's presence with praise,
enter with shouting and song.

PSALM 95:1-2

MORNING READING

By a joyful face, therefore, he understood fervour, thoughtfulness, and the disposition and preparation of mind and body to a ready undertaking of every good work; for this fervour and readiness often have a greater influence on people than by the good deed itself. Indeed, however good an action may be, if it does not seem to have been done willingly and fervently, it tends to produce distaste rather than edification.

MIRROR OF PERFECTION

As there is an evil zeal of bitterness which separates from God and leads to hell, so there is a good zeal which separates from vices and leads to God and life everlasting. Let monks, therefore, practice this latter zeal with most fervent love: that is, let them in honor anticipate one another; let them bear most patiently one another's infirmities, whether of body or of character; let them endeavor to surpass one another in the practice of mutual obedience; let no one seek that which he accounts useful for himself, but rather what is profitable to another; let them practice fraternal charity with a chaste love; let them fear God; let them love their Abbot with a sincere and humble affection; let them prefer nothing whatever to Christ; and may he bring us all alike to life everlasting. Amen.

THE HOLY RULE OF SAINT BENEDICT

FOR REFLECTION

How easy to become disheartened and focused on myself, forgetting that my attitude affects those around me. The world is full of people whose hearts are weighted with sorrow and hurt, who long to experience the happiness and peace that you offer.

Holy One, fill me with the spirit of joy in your service and in the service of your people. Help me put others' needs before my own, and bear patiently the difficulties and trials of life. In all endeavors, large and small, at home and on the job, bless me with a willing spirit. Infused with gladness, let my enthusiasm for your work lead others to you.

EVENING READING

Blessed Francis used to say, "Although I know that the devils envy me the blessings that God has given me, I also know and see that they cannot harm me through myself, so they plan and try to hurt me through my companions. But if they cannot hurt me either through myself or through my companions, they retire in great confusion. Indeed, whenever I am tempted or depressed, if I see my companions joyful, I immediately turn away from my temptation and oppression, and regain my own inward and outward joy.

"For what are God's servants but his minstrels," he said, "who must inspire the hearts of men and stir them to spiritual joy."

Mirror of Perfection

Mary, Tabernacle of the Lord, Lead Us to Your Son

I show you the path to walk.
As your teacher,
I watch out for you.

PSALM 32:8

MORNING READING

Toward the Mother of Jesus he was filled with an inexpressible love, because it was she who made the Lord of Majesty our brother. He sang special *Praises* to her, poured out prayers to her, offered her his affections, so many and so great that the tongue of man cannot recount them. But what delights us most, he made her the advocate of the order and placed under her wings the sons he was about to leave that she might cherish them and protect them to the end.

THOMAS OF CELANO, *THE SECOND LIFE OF ST. FRANCIS*

Heart of Mary, sacred temple,
Tabernacle of the Lord—
House of God, his sanctuary,
Silence holding God the Word—
There the Spirit rests complacent;
There His royal court doth hold;
Thence come treasures ever flowing.
Heart of Mary, House of Gold.

"HYMN TO THE IMMACULATE HEART OF MARY"

FOR REFLECTION

Holy Mary, keep me in your heart and in your care. As you have been, I long to be: handmaid, servant of the Lord.

EVENING READING

Hail, holy Lady,
Chosen by the most holy Father in heaven,
  Consecrated by him,
   With his most holy beloved Son
   And the Holy Spirit, the Comforter.
On you descended and in you still remains
   All the fulness of grace
   And every good.
Hail, his Palace.
Hail, his Tabernacle.
Hail, his Robe.
Hail, his Handmaid.
Hail, his Mother.
And Hail, all holy Virtues,
   Who, by the grace
   And inspiration of the Holy Spirit,
   Are poured into the hearts of the faithful
   So that, faithless no longer,
   They may be made faithful servants of God
   Through you.

SALUTATION OF THE BLESSED VIRGIN

What Joy to Have Such a Brother in Heaven

With a heart full of thanks
I proclaim your wonders, God.
You are my joy, my delight;
I sing hymns to your name, Most High.

PSALM 9:2-3

MORNING READING

Intoxicated by love and compassion for Christ, blessed Francis sometimes used to act in ways like these. For the sweetest of spiritual melodies would often well up within him and found expression in French melodies, and the murmurs of God's voice, heard by him alone, would joyfully pour forth in the French tongue.

Sometimes he would pick up a stick from the ground, and laying it on his left arm, he would draw another stick across it with his right hand like a bow, as though he were playing a viol or some other instrument; and he would imitate the movements of a musician and sing in French of our Lord Jesus Christ.

MIRROR OF PERFECTION

Come, let us join our cheerful songs
  With angels round the throne;
Ten thousand thousand are their tongues,
  But all their joys are one.
The whole creation join in one
To bless the sacred name
Of him that sits upon the throne,
And to adore the Lamb.

ISAAC WATTS

"CHRIST JESUS, THE LAMB OF GOD WORSHIPPED BY ALL CREATION"

FOR REFLECTION

O, Wellspring of Life, sometimes the exuberance of your love fills my heart to overflowing. In the midst of such abundance I lift my voice with Francis, with the saints and angels, with my sisters and brothers on earth, to praise your name.

EVENING READING

How glorious, how holy and wonderful it is to have a Father in heaven. How holy it is, how beautiful and lovable to have in heaven a Bridegroom. How holy and beloved, how pleasing and lowly, how peaceful, delightful, lovable and desirable above all things it is to have a Brother like this, who laid down his life for his sheep (cf. Jn 10:15), and prayed to his Father for us, saying: Holy Father, in your name keep those whom you have given me. Father, all those whom you gave me in the world, were yours and you gave them to me. And the words you have given me, I have given to them. And they have received them and have known truly that I have come forth from you, and they have believed that you have sent me. I am praying for them, not for the world; Bless and sanctify them. And for them I sanctify myself, that they may be sanctified in their unity, just as we are. And, Father, I wish that where I am, they also may be with me, that they may see my splendor in your kingdom (cf. Jn 17:6-24).

LETTER TO ALL THE FAITHFUL

We Find Joy in Living for God Alone

You give my heart more joy
than all their grain and wine.
I sleep secure at night,
you keep me in your care.

PSALM 4:8-9

[Editor's note: Unable to change Francis' mind by his own means,
his father took him before the bishop, hoping to make Francis return
all his money, and renounce any claims on the family's wealth and
position.]

MORNING READING

In his genuine love for poverty, Francis was more than ready to
comply and he willingly appeared before the bishop. There he
made no delay—without hesitation, without hearing or saying a
word—he immediately took off his clothes and gave them back to
his father. Then it was discovered that he wore a hair-shirt under
his fine clothes next to his skin. He even took off his trousers in
his fervor and enthusiasm and stood there naked before them all.
Then he said to his father, "Until now I called you my father, but
from now on I can say without reserve, 'Our Father who art in
heaven.' He is all my wealth and I place all my confidence in him."
When the bishop heard this, he was amazed at his passionate fervor. He jumped to his feet and took Francis into his embrace, cov-
ering him with the cloak he was wearing, like the good man that
he was. Then he told his servants to bring some clothes for him
and they gave him an old tunic which belonged to one of the
bishop's farmhands. Francis took it gratefully and drew a cross on

it with his own hand with a piece of chalk, making it a worthy garment for a man who was crucified and a beggar. And so the servant of the most high King was left stripped of all that belonged to him, that he might follow the Lord whom he loved, who hung naked on the cross.

ST. BONAVENTURE, MAJOR LIFE OF ST. FRANCIS

He was penniless, he was parentless, he was to all appearance without a trade or a plan or a hope in the world; and as he went under the frosty trees, he burst suddenly into song.

G.K. CHESTERTON

FOR REFLECTION

Ever Watchful God, dispel the fears that linger in my heart and keep me from such abandon. The more I am able, by your grace, to give my life to you, the more your joy will fill my soul.

EVENING READING

And so we must all keep close watch over ourselves or we will be lost and turn our minds and hearts from God, because we think there is something worth having or doing, or that we will gain some advantage.

In that love which is God (cf. 1 Jn 4:16), I entreat all my friars, ministers and subjects, to put away every attachment, all care and solicitude, and serve, love, honor, and adore our Lord and God with a pure heart and mind; this is what he seeks above all else.

THE RULE OF 1221

We Should Praise God Always With All Our Hearts

Praise the Lord, my heart!
My whole life, give praise.

PSALM 146:1

MORNING READING

This saint indeed had labored assiduously in the Lord's vineyard, untiringly fervent in prayer, fasting, vigils, and preaching; he had walked in paths leading to salvation, caring attentively for his fellow men in watchful compassion and in humble disregard for himself. All this he had done from the beginning of his conversion until he departed to Christ whom he had loved with his whole heart, with whom his mind was always filled, whom he praised continually with his voice and glorified in his works. He loved God so fervently that it sufficed for Francis to hear him named to be so fired with love that his whole person glowed and he broke into the words: "At the name of God the heavens and earth should bow down."

LEGEND OF THE THREE COMPANIONS

[Editor's note: Seventeenth-century Carmelite Brother Lawrence was renowned for his holiness and simple way of prayer often called "The practice of the presence of God." The following story was told of Brother Lawrence as he lay on his deathbed.]

When a monk asked him what he was doing and what was occupying his mind, he replied: "I am doing what I will do throughout all eternity. I am blessing God, I am praising God, and I am adoring and loving him with all my heart. This sums up our entire call and duty, brothers: to adore God and to love him without worrying about the rest."

BROTHER LAWRENCE

FOR REFLECTION

God Who Waits, you accept our songs and prayers of praise, yet it is our hearts you most desire. Help me gather myself into the depths of my heart, so I can send from there my hymns of exultation.

[Editor's note: The following excerpt from the prayer, The Praises, was composed, as were many of St. Francis' prayers, of selections from Scripture and the liturgy. It is thought that this prayer was recited often during the day by Francis and his friars.]

EVENING READING

"Bless the Lord, all you works of the Lord" (Dn 3:57).

R. Let us praise and glorify him for ever.

"Praise our God, all you his servants,

and you who fear him, the small and the great" (Rv 19:5).

R. Let us praise and glorify him for ever.

Praise him in his glory, heaven and earth, "and every creature that is in heaven and on the earth and under the earth, and such as are on the sea, and all that are in them." (Rv 5:13).

R. Let us praise and glorify him for ever.

Prayer

All-powerful, all holy, most high and supreme God, sovereign good, all good, every good, you who alone are good, it is to you we must give all praise, all glory, all thanks, all honor, all blessing; to you we must refer all good always. Amen.

THE PRAISES BEFORE THE OFFICE

Prayers of St. Francis of Assisi

These prayers are followed by the page number
where they can be found in *St. Francis of Assisi:
Writings and Early Biographies: English Omnibus of
the Sources for the Life of St. Francis.*

PRAISES OF THE BLESSED VIRGIN

I greet you, Lady, holy Queen,
    holy Mary, Mother of God,
    Virgin who became the Church,
    chosen by the most holy Father
    of heaven;
    consecrated to holiness
    through his most holy and beloved
    Son and the Holy Spirit,
    the Comforter;
    in you was and is
    the whole fullness of grace
    and everything that is good.
I greet you, his princely dwelling.
I greet you, the tent of his covenant.
I greet you, his habitation.
I greet you, his garment.
I greet you, his handmaid.
I greet you, his mother,
    with all holy virtues, which
    through the grace and light of the
    Holy Spirit descend unto the hearts
    of believers
    to make believers of unbelievers
    for God.

(1925-26)

PRAISES OF GOD

You are holy, Lord, the only God,
      and your deeds are wonderful.
You are strong.
      You are great.
      You are the Most High,
      You are almighty.
      You, holy Father, are
      King of heaven and earth.
You are Three and One,
      Lord God, all good.
      You are Good, all Good, supreme Good,
      Lord God, living and true.
You are love,
      You are wisdom.
      You are humility,
      You are endurance.
      You are rest,
      You are peace.
      You are joy and gladness.
      You are justice and moderation.
      You are all our riches,
      And you suffice for us.
You are beauty.
      You are gentleness.
      You are our protector,
      You are our guardian and defender.
      You are our courage.
      You are our haven and our hope.
You are our faith,

Our great consolation.
You are our eternal life,
Great and wonderful Lord,
God almighty,
Merciful Savior.

(125)

THE SAN DAMIANO PRAYER

Most high and glorious God, lighten the darkness of my
heart and give me sound faith, firm hope, and perfect love.
Let me, Lord, have the right feelings and knowledge, so
that I can carry out the task that you have given me in truth.

(1916-17)

THE CANTICLE OF BROTHER SUN

Most high, all-powerful, all good Lord!
All praise is yours, all glory, all honor
And all blessing.
To you, alone, Most High, do they belong.
No mortal lips are worthy
To pronounce your name.
All praise be yours, my Lord, through all that you have made,
And first my lord Brother Sun,
Who brings the day; and light you give us through him.
How beautiful is he, how radiant in all his splendor!
Of you, Most High, he bears the likeness.

All praise be yours, my Lord, through Sister Moon and Stars;
  In the heavens you have made them, bright
  And precious and fair.
All praise be yours, my Lord, through Brothers Wind and Air,
  And fair and stormy, all the weather's moods,
  By which you cherish all that you have made.
All praise be yours, my Lord, through Sister Water,
  So useful, lowly, precious and pure.
All praise be yours, my Lord, through Brother Fire,
  Through whom you brighten up the night.
  How beautiful is he, how gay! Full of power and strength.
All praise be yours, my Lord, through Sister Earth, our
  mother,
  Who feeds us in her sovereignty and produces
  Various fruits with colored flowers and herbs.
All praise be yours, my Lord, through those who grant pardon
  For love of you; through those who endure
  Sickness and trial.
Happy those who endure in peace,
  By you, Most High, they will be crowned.
All praise be yours, my Lord, through Sister Death,
  From whose embrace no mortal can escape.
Woe to those who die in mortal sin!
  Happy those She finds doing your will!
  The second death can do no harm to them.
Praise and bless my Lord, and give him thanks,
  And serve him with great humility.

(130-31)

NOTES

Readings

1. Marion A. Habig, *St. Francis of Assisi, Writings and Early Biographies: English Omnibus of the Sources for the Life of Saint Francis* (Chicago: Franciscan Press, 1983), 1056; Catherine de Hueck Doherty, *Poustinia: Christian Spirituality of the East for Western Man* (Notre Dame, Ind.: Ave Maria, 1975), 26–27; Habig, 49.

2. Habig, 233–34; Thomas Merton, *Thoughts in Solitude* (New York: Farrar, Straus and Giroux, 1956, 1958), 83; Habig, 108.

3. Habig, 1874 (From *A New Fioretti: A Collection of Early Stories About St. Francis of Assisi,* John R.H. Moorman, trans. This is also found in the Omnibus of Sources.); Austin Flannery, ed., *Vatican Council II: The Conciliar and Post Conciliar Documents* (Northport, N.Y.: Costello, 1975), 762, 764; Habig, 448.

4. Habig, 1139–40; Brother Lawrence, *The Practice of the Presence of God,* Robert J. Edmonson, trans. (Orleans, Mass.: Paraclete, 1985), 89–90; Habig, 440.

5. Habig, 288; Habig, 1275. (This is from Raphael Brown's introduction to "Little Flowers of St. Francis," included in the Omnibus of Sources.); Habig, 1608. (Jacques de Vitry's Letter, 1216 R.B.C. Huygens, Lettres de Jacques de Vitry, Edition Critique, Leyde, 1960, 75–76. This is also in the Omnibus of Sources.)

6. Habig, 811; St. Basil, *Long Rules, Q. 37, Ascetical Works* (New York, 1950), as quoted in Thomas Merton, *Contemplative Prayer* (New York: Herder and Herder, 1969), 35; Habig, 52.

7. Habig, 465–66; Habig, 1014–15.

8. Habig, 47–48; *Catechism of the Catholic Church* (Dubuque, Iowa: Brown ROA, 1994), 658; Habig, 706.

9. Habig, 232; Francis Thompson, *The Hound of Heaven* (Harrisburg: Morehouse, 1996), 4–7. (First published in Great Britain in 1947.); Habig, 637–38.

10. Habig, 1875–76; Marie Dennis, Joseph Nangle, Cynthia Moe-Lobeda, Stuart Taylor, *St. Francis and the Foolishness of God* (Maryknoll, N.Y.: Orbis, 1993), 147; Habig, 441.

11. Habig, 680; Omer Englebert, *St. Francis of Assisi: A Biography* (Ann Arbor, Mich.: Servant, 1979), 72; Habig, 419.

12. Habig, 434–35; Mother Teresa, *Whatever You Did Unto One of the Least, You Did Unto Me* from the National Prayer Breakfast, Washington, D.C., February 1994 www.fn.net/~bbrown/sr/mother.html; Habig, 1160.

13. Habig, 232; Charlotte Elliott, "The Lamb of God," in Ian Bradley, ed., *The Book of Hymns* (Woodstock, N.Y.: Overlook, 1989), 229; Habig, 317–18.

14. Habig, 1079–80; St. Frances de Sales; Habig, 84.

15. Habig, 673; William Johnston, ed., *The Cloud of Unknowing and The Book of Privy Counseling* (New York: Doubleday, 1973), 156; Habig, 1863.

16. Habig, 231–32; Abba Poemen, as quoted in Benedicta Ward, ed. and trans., *The Desert Christian: Sayings of the Desert Fathers: The Alphabetical Collection* (New York: Macmillan, 1979), 178; Habig, 233.

17. Habig, 680–81; Walter Hilton, *The Scale of Perfection* (A new translation, made using the 1927 version [London: Burns, Oates & Washbourne] and that by Gerard Sitwell [London: Burns & Oates, 1953] as found in Gordon L. Miller, *The Way of the English Mystics: An Anthology and Guide for Pilgrims* (Ridgefield, Conn.: Morehouse, 1996), 54; Habig, 38.

18. Habig, 657–58; St. Thérèse of Lisieux as quoted in John A. Hardon, ed., *The Treasury of Catholic Wisdom* (San Francisco: Ignatius, 1995 (original publication 1987 Doubleday),632; Habig, 921.

19. Habig, 1210–11; St. Catherine of Siena, *Dialogue*, as quoted in Hardon, 346; Habig, 1156.

20. Habig, 230–31; Habig, 110.

21. Habig, 720–21; Pope Benedict XV; Habig, 722.

22. Habig, 490; St. Benedict, *The Holy Rule of Our Most Holy Father Saint Benedict*, Benedictine Monks of St. Meinrad Archabbey, ed. (St. Meinrad, Ind.: Abbey, 1975), 2; Habig, 37–38.

23. Habig, 724–25; Habig, 1080.

24. Habig, 703–4; Brother Charles de Foucauld. Jean-François Six, ed., J. Holland Smith, trans., *Spiritual Autobiography of Charles de Foucauld* (New York: P.J. Kenedy & Sons, 1964), 23; Habig, 725.

25. Habig, 646–47; Dorothy Day, *Letter on Hospices*, on "Dorothy Day Library on the Web" at www.catholicworker.org/dorothyday/ originally in *The Catholic Worker*, Jan. 1948, 2.8; Habig, 247.

26. Habig, 711–12; St. Richard of Chichester; Habig, 81.

27. Habig, 237–38; Esther de Waal, *A Seven Day Journey With Thomas Merton* (Ann Arbor, Mich.: Servant, 1992), 51; Habig, 1234.

28. Habig, 670; John Henry Newman, "Lead Kindly Light," in Bradley, 235; Habig, 495.

29. Habig, 638–39; Esther de Waal, ed., *The Celtic Vision: Prayers and Blessings from the Outer Hebrides* (Petersham, Mass.: St. Bede's, 1988), 31; Habig, 654–55.

30. Habig, 1328; Julian of Norwich, *Showings*, Edmund Colledge and James Walsh, eds. (New York: Paulist, 1978), 130–31; Habig, 1140.

31. Habig, 370–71; Habig, 953.

32. Habig, 1235; *Psalm XI*, in Bradley, 46; Habig, 318–19.

33. Habig, 907; Edward Hays, *Pray All Ways* (Easton, Kan.: Forest of Peace, 1981), 92; Habig, 81.

34. Habig, 421; G.K. Chesterton, *St. Francis of Assisi* (Garden City, N.Y.: Doubleday, 1957), 52; Habig, 912–13.

35. Habig, 942–43; St. Basil the Great of Caesarea; Habig, 364.

36. Habig, 700–701; John Vianney as quoted in Joe H. Adels, *The Wisdom of the Saints: The Anthology of Voices* (New York: Oxford University Press, 1987), 16; Habig, 892.

37. Habig, 1060; de Foucauld, 57; Habig, 925.

38. Habig, 475–76; Habig, 80.

39. Habig, 1332; Henri Nouwen, *Bread for the Journey*, as quoted in Madeleine L'Engle and Luci Shaw, *Friends for the Journey* (Ann Arbor, Mich.: Servant, 1997), 133; Habig, 1332–33.

40. Habig, 72; Julian of Norwich, 296, 299; Habig, 1154.

41. Habig, 292–93; St. John the Almsgiver; Habig, 400–401.

42. Habig, 635–36; Flannery, 776; Habig, 95.

43. Habig, 1064–65; St. Fulgentius; Habig, 82.

44. Habig, 809; Habig, 1063.

45. Habig, 1881–82 (Wadding, Annales Minorum, 24–25, as quoted in

Habig); Folliott Sandford Pierpoint, "All Things Bright and Beautiful," in Bradley, 30; Habig, 696.

46. Habig, 1256–57; St. Cyril of Jerusalem, *Lecture XVI* as found on *Christian Classic Ethereal Library* server, at Wheaton College, ccel.wheaton.edu/fathers2/NPNF2-07/Npnf2-07-21.htm#p2201 621653; Habig, 130.

47. Habig, 698; Chesterton, 76; Habig, 45.

48. Habig, 1257; St. Felix of Cantalice; St. Nicodemus; Habig, 808.

49. Habig, 296; de Waal, *The Celtic Vision,* 29; Habig, 97.

50. Habig, 296–97; Mary van Balen Holt, *All Earth Is Crammed With Heaven: Daily Reflections for Mothers* (Ann Arbor, Mich.: Servant, 1996), 164; Habig, 1252.

51. Habig, 442; Madeleine L'Engle, *Penguins + Golden Calves: Icons and Idols* (Wheaton, Ill.: Harold Shaw, 1996), 14, 19; Habig, 299–300.

52. Habig, 1257; Thomas Merton, *New Seeds of Contemplation* (New York: New Directions, 1961), 29–30; Habig, 1021.

53. Habig, 1501–2; Isaac Watts, "When I Survey the Wondrous Cross," in Bradley, 454; Habig, 1847–48.

54. Habig, 50–52; Dorothy Day, *From Union Square to Rome* (chapter 2–Childhood, 18–27, from "Dorothy Day Library on the Web" at URL: www.catholicworker.org/dorothyday/; Habig, 1258.

55. Habig, 465; Anne Gordon, *A Book of Saints* (New York: Bantam, 1994), 125; Habig, 920.

56. Habig, 1231; St. Benedict, 89; Habig, 1230, 1236.

57. Habig, 521; Carmel Bride, "Hymn To the Immaculate Heart of Mary," in *As Milk Is Poured* (Paterson, N.J.: St. Anthony Guild, 1957), 39; Habig, 135–36.

58. Habig, 1226; Isaac Watts, "Christ Jesus, the Lamb of God Worshipped by All Creation," in Bradley, 95; Habig, 96–97.

59. Habig, 642–43; Chesterton, 56; Habig, 48–49.

60. Habig, 952–53; Brother Lawrence, 55; Habig, 138–39.